Simply
Word for
Windows

Robert Kermish

Osborne **McGraw-Hill**
2600 Tenth Street
Berkeley, California 94710
U.S.A.

For information on translations or book distributors outside of the U.S.A., please write to Osborne **McGraw-Hill** at the above address.

Simply Word for Windows

1234567890 DOC 99876543

ISBN 0-07-881888-5

Acknowledgments

The process of creating a book takes a tremendous amount of teamwork and coordination. The words written by the author are only the first step in bringing a book to completion.

The people I worked with at Osborne/McGraw-Hill are talented and creative. I would like to thank Frances Stack for all of her guidance and assistance throughout this entire project. Jill Pisoni was always there to keep me on track and listen to my corny jokes. Her reminders of when chapters were due will be forever burned into my memory. The suggestions and modifications by Laura Sackerman, Kelly Barr, and Kathyrn Hashimoto were right on the money. The artwork created by Marla Shelasky and the page layouts designed by Fred Lass complete the loop by making the writing come to life. The technical editing provided by Leigh Yafa was top notch.

All of my friends and family have been very supportive and gave me large doses of encouragement. I want to mention my father, who would have been the proudest dad of all if he was here to see his son's book. Lastly, my thanks to my wife Marsha who gave me all her love. I couldn't have done this book without her.

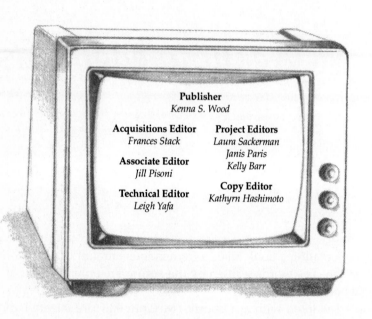

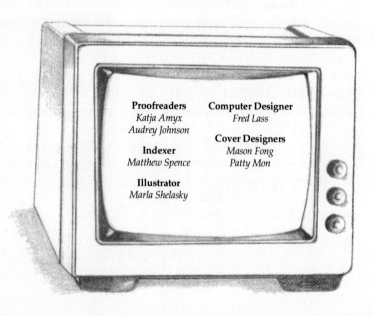

Contents

It's Simple to Use This Lay-Flat Binding ...

Open this book to any page you choose and crease back the left-hand page by pressing along the length of the spine with your fingers. Now, the book will stay open until you're ready to go on to another page.

Unlike regular book bindings, this special binding won't weaken or crack when you crease back the pages. It's tough, durable, and resilient—designed to withstand years of daily use. So go ahead, put this book to the test and use it as often as you like.

Introduction to Word for Windows

Welcome to *Simply Word for Windows*. You are about to learn the basics you will need to use Word for Windows on a daily basis. If you need to type a letter, make some changes, save it, and then print it, you are in the right place. You'll also have the opportunity to pick up other skills, such as bolding text and automatically putting page numbers on each page. This book is set up to allow you to turn to the chapter that will give you specific steps to accomplish the tasks you need.

The most important thing to remember is to relax and enjoy using this program. Do as much as you feel comfortable with, then come back to it another time to learn more.

A Brief Note on Word Processing

Until the early 1970s, the only ways to put words on paper were to handwrite them, use a typewriter, or use a printing press. Changing typewritten words meant retyping the text or using a lot of correction fluid. With the development of electronic word processors, the ability to make changes on the fly added greater flexibility. Those early machines were called *dedicated word processors* because they performed only one function—word processing. Today's computers can do many more types of functions, of which word processing is just one.

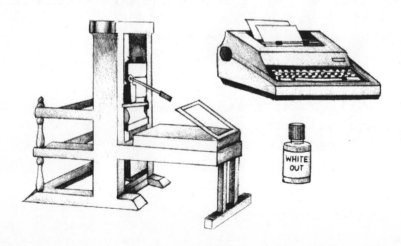

What Is a Word Processor?

A word processor is a computer program that allows you to type words which appear on the computer screen. You can create memos, letters, reports, or any document that you could write by hand. Once the words are entered, you can easily make changes, such as moving sentences or deleting words. This feature is called *editing*. You can also enhance the appearance of text, such as adding italics or underlines. This feature is called *formatting*.

Word for Windows goes beyond just basic editing and formatting. If you need to save the document to continue working on it another time, Word for Windows will save the text on the computer hard disk or a floppy disk. If you're not the world's best speller, Word for Windows has a feature called *spelling* that will pause at misspelled words and even offer suggestions to help make corrections. A *thesaurus* is also available that offers synonyms to keep you from repeating the same words.

Once you are satisfied with your document, Word for Windows can print one or more copies of it on a printer. You can even tell Word for Windows which specific pages to print.

Here is the standard procedure to create a document:

1. Type on the keyboard to enter text on the screen.
2. Edit the text to arrange it the way you want.
3. Format the document as needed.
4. Tell the program to check for spelling errors.
5. Print the document on a printer.

6. Save the document to your hard disk or a floppy disk, if you want to recall it later.

Starting the Computer

To use Word for Windows, you must first turn on your computer and monitor, as well as the printer (if you want to print out your text). The term *boot up* the computer is commonly used and also means starting the computer.

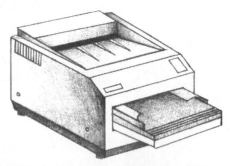

Note: *Before you turn the computer on, remove any floppy disks from the disk drives. If you leave a floppy disk in the drive, it may prevent DOS (and Windows) from loading, which will cause an error message to display.*

What Is DOS?

When you switch on your computer, a special program called DOS starts up. DOS stands for Disk Operating System. It allows you to type commands to start up other programs. DOS is also the program that allows Word for Windows to save your documents on disk as well as to print your documents on a printer. As the computer starts up, some numbers might show at the top of your screen. The computer is checking the amount of RAM that is built into it.

RAM stands for Random Access Memory. This is the electronic memory that holds Word for Windows while you are creating a document. When you *launch*, or start, Word for Windows, the Word for Windows program is copied from your hard disk into RAM so you can use Word's many commands.

In most cases, when DOS is finished loading, you will see a C> or C:\> on your screen. This is called the the *DOS prompt*. For more information about DOS, refer to *Simply DOS* by Kris Jamsa (Berkeley, CA: Osborne/McGraw-Hill, 1991).

Note: If your computer is set up to automatically launch Windows when the computer starts up, the first thing you will see onscreen after the RAM numbers is the Windows logo. After a few seconds, the Windows hourglass appears to let you know that Windows will finish loading in just a few moments. When Windows has finished loading, you will see Windows' Program Manager window. You will not see the DOS prompt at all.

Starting Windows

Once the DOS prompt is on your screen, you are ready to start Microsoft Windows.

Note: If your computer starts up Windows automatically, you do not have to perform the following steps.

1. Type cd\windows and press the ENTER key.

2. Type win and press ENTER again.

If you see an error message such as "Bad command or file name," you need to check if Windows has been installed or if it is installed on a different drive.

What Is Microsoft Windows?

Microsoft Windows has what computer people call a *graphical user interface,* or GUI (pronounced "gooey"). What this means in plain English is that you see pictures, or *icons,* on your screen to represent programs and documents. On DOS-type computers without Windows, you need to type a command to launch a program. Windows allows you to start programs by using the mouse. You point at an icon with the mouse pointer and then click the mouse button to select the icon. For more material concerning Microsoft Windows, refer to *Simply Windows* by Mary Campbell (Berkeley, CA: Osborne/McGraw-Hill, 1992).

When Windows finishes *loading,* or starting up, the Program Manager appears on your screen. You use the Program Manager to start software programs and organize the programs and documents into groups that make sense to you.

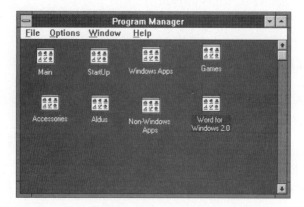

Starting Word for Windows

To launch Word for Windows, you need first to open the program group that contains the Word for Windows application. A *program group* contains the icons for an application and files associated with that application. (The terms *application, software program,* and *program* are interchangeable.) Once the program group is open, then the application can be started up.

One of the program groups on your screen should be named Word for Windows 2.0. To open it, move the mouse so that the tip of the arrow on your screen is pointing at the Word for Windows program group, then *double-click* (two rapid clicks of the left mouse button); try not to move the mouse while you double-click.

Tip: If double-clicking doesn't work, click once on the Word for Windows program group and press ENTER. *(The Control menu for the program group might appear, but pressing* ENTER *makes the menu disappear.)*

The Control menu

Once the Word for Windows program group is open, you see all the items it contains.

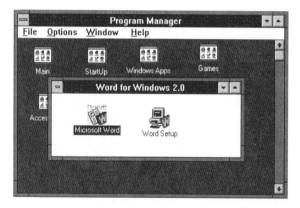

Now you're ready to start Word for Windows. Double-click (or click once and press ENTER) the Microsoft Word icon. A small hourglass appears on the screen, indicating that the program is loading and will take just a few more seconds before you can get down to business.

The Word for Windows Screen

So here you are, with the computer equivalent of a blank piece of paper staring at you, waiting for you to type something. Before you start typing, take a look at a few of the items on the screen.

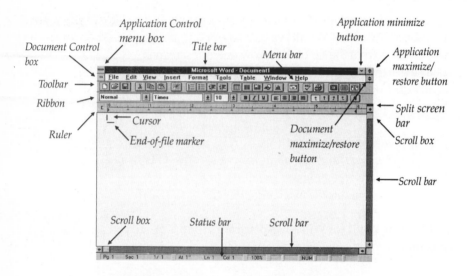

Application Control menu box — Title bar — Menu bar — Application minimize button — Application maximize/restore button — Document Control box — Toolbar — Ribbon — Ruler — Cursor — End-of-file marker — Document maximize/restore button — Split screen bar — Scroll box — Scroll bar — Scroll box — Status bar — Scroll bar

Title Bar

The *title bar* is where Word for Windows shows the name of the document you're working with. Because you haven't named the document yet, Word for Windows assigns it the name Document1. You will learn in Chapter 2 how to save and name your documents.

Menu Bar

The *menu bar* shows the menus in Word for Windows. To access the different menus, point the mouse at one of the menu names and click the left mouse button. The menu bar will be covered in Chapter 2.

Control Menu Boxes

At the extreme left side of the title bar is the *application Control menu box*. Clicking this box opens the application Control menu, which allows you to resize, move, or close Word for Windows. At the far left side of the menu bar is the *document Control menu box*. When you click this box, the document

Control menu opens, which helps you resize, move, or close the active document. For further information, consult your Windows documentation.

Minimize and Maximize/Restore Buttons

In the upper-right corner of the screen are three buttons: the *application minimize button, application maximize/restore button,* and *document maximize/restore button.* These buttons allow the resizing of the program window and the document window. They are discussed further in Chapter 5.

Note: The program window contains the application that is presently loaded. This is also sometimes called an application window. The document window contains the current document. The document window is within the program window.

Toolbar

The *toolbar* is located directly below the menu bar. It has icons that perform specific tasks when selected. You can click an icon to save a file or start the spelling, instead of using menus to access these commands. These items will be covered in Chapter 10.

Ribbon

The *ribbon*, beneath the toolbar, allows "one-step" formatting of your documents. As you will learn in Chapter 10, formatting your words is a great way to enhance and emphasize certain parts of your document.

Ruler

The *ruler* is displayed beneath the ribbon. It shows the present paragraph and tab settings. The ruler will be covered in Chapter 8.

Cursor and End-of-File Marker

The blinking *cursor* shows your current position within the document. As you type, the cursor moves to the right. The *end-of-file marker* tells you there is no text past this point. No text can appear past this mark.

Status Bar

The *status bar*, at the bottom of the screen, indicates the current position of the cursor in the document. It also tells you, for example, if your CAPS LOCK or NUM LOCK keys are on. Notice that the word "NUM" is visible at the bottom right in the screen shown earlier in this chapter. This means that the NUM LOCK key is on. The word "CAPS" appears to the left of "NUM" if the CAPS LOCK key is depressed.

Scroll Bars and Scroll Boxes

The horizontal and vertical *scroll bars* allow you to access items that may not be currently visible on your screen. Scrolling capability will become very handy when you create a document that is longer than one page. The *scroll box* currently appears at the top of the vertical scroll bar, as well as the far left of the horizontal scroll bar, which means that you are viewing the top and far left side of the document. If you type a file longer than one screen, the vertical scroll box moves down to signal that you are now past viewing the top of your document.

Note: Using the scroll bars with no text on the screen performs no useful function. Since there is no text yet, the beginning and ending of the file are at the same place, and your screen view doesn't change. Once there is some text on the screen, the scroll bars have a useful purpose.

Split Screen Bar

The *split screen bar* is just above the up arrow in the vertical scroll bar. As you will learn in Chapter 5, the split screen bar allows you to compare different parts of the same document at the same time.

Mousing Around

The mouse is important when using Word for Windows. It is, for example, the only way to access the scroll bars and scroll boxes. You can use the mouse to select commands from the menu, the toolbar, and the ribbon, as well as to move items on the ruler.

Using the Mouse

To use the mouse properly, position it so its cord is facing away from you, and rest your fingers on the buttons. Put the mouse on a flat surface so the pointer moves smoothly across the screen. If your desk is very smooth, you should consider purchasing a mouse pad. It gives the mouse the friction it needs to move the pointer consistently on the screen. You place the mouse pad on the desk and put the mouse on the mouse pad.

Moving the mouse in any direction (except lifting it off your desk) moves the pointer on the screen. Depending on the manufacturer, the mouse usually has two buttons; Word for Windows primarily uses the left button. If you run out of room at the edge of your desk as you mouse around, just pick up the mouse and set it down somewhere away from the edge.

As you move the mouse around, the pointer representing the mouse changes on the screen depending on where it is. If it is in the middle of the typing area, the mouse pointer looks like a capital letter I, called an *I-beam*. If you are pointing at a menu, the mouse pointer becomes an arrow pointing up and to the left. If you move the mouse pointer to the extreme left side of the typing area (called the *selection area*), it becomes an arrow pointing up and to the right. This last pointer will be discussed further in Chapter 4.

Selecting a Menu Item

Word for Windows commands are usually accessed by pointing at one of the nine menus and clicking the left mouse button. After you click, a drop-down menu appears with several commands. Point to the command you want to use and click it. (If any of the menu commands are dimmed, then they are not available at this time.)

File	
New...	
Open...	Ctrl+F12
Close	
Save	Shift+F12
Save As...	F12
Save All	
Find File...	
Summary Info...	
Template...	
Print Preview	
Print...	Ctrl+Shift+F12
Print Merge...	
Print Setup...	
Exit	Alt+F4
1 RAFTING2.DOC	
2 VIRGINIA.DOC	
3 A:\SUPER.MEM	
4 B:\CHAP6.DOC	

Tip: If you have clicked the wrong menu, just click the correct menu or, to return to the document, click anywhere outside the active menu and beneath the ruler. If you select the wrong command and a dialog box appears, click the Cancel button to return to the document.

Function Keys

Located across the top of your keyboard or down the left side are some keys called the function keys. Depending on the type of keyboard, the function keys will be numbered F1 to F10 or F1 to F12. These keys direct Word for Windows to carry out specific commands. For example, pressing F5, the Goto key, enables you to jump quickly to a certain page in your document.

Keyboard Equivalents

The function keys can perform the same actions as using the mouse to click a menu command. These are called *keyboard equivalents*. The keys are used by themselves, or in conjunction with the CTRL, SHIFT, or ALT keys, which are called *booster keys*.

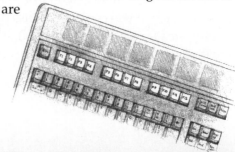

To help you remember the different keyboard equivalent commands, Microsoft supplies a plastic template that sits at the top of the keyboard. Each function key can be used to select as many as six commands, when combined with the booster keys.

If a desired command requires using a function key plus a booster key, don't try to press both keys simultaneously—your left hand is not racing with your right. Press and hold down the booster key first, and then press the function key. For example, the keyboard equivalent to quit Word for Windows is CTRL-F4, which means you press and hold down CTRL with either hand and then press F4. If the command requires two booster keys (for example, the keyboard equivalent for Print is CTRL-SHIFT-F12), hold the two booster keys down together (preferably with the same hand), then press the function key.

Another Keyboard Method

There is another way to use the keyboard to open menus and select commands. If you look closely at the menu bar items, you will notice that a single letter within each word is underlined. If you press the ALT key and then press the letter that is underlined in a menu name, the menu opens. Notice that each command in a menu also has a single letter underlined. If you press this underlined letter, the command's dialog box opens. Dialog boxes are covered in Chapter 2.

Keyboard or Mouse?

You should activate commands in the style that is most comfortable for you. If you prefer using the mouse more, or if you find using the keyboard equivalents or ALT key method easier, then *that's* the right way. Word for Windows commands can be accessed whichever way works best for you.

What Do They Mean By...?

A computer program that allows you to type words, using a keyboard, and have the words appear on the computer screen.

Load   Another word for launch or start up. For example, the computer loads, or starts up, DOS when you switch it on. To load, or launch, Windows, type **win** at the DOS prompt.

DOS   Stands for Disk Operating System. DOS allows you to type in commands to start up software programs.

RAM   Stands for Random Access Memory. This is the electronic memory that "holds" Word for Windows while you are writing a document.

Microsoft Windows   A program with a graphical user interface. This means you will see pictures on your screen to represent software programs and the documents you create using them.

Icon   Another word for the pictures you see when Microsoft Windows is active.

Menu Bar   The horizontal list of commands at the top of a document window.

Drop-Down Menu   A vertical list of commands that appears when you select a menu bar command.

Function Keys   The block of keys on the keyboard marked F1 to F12, or F1 to F10.

Keyboard Equivalent   Using a function key to access a command instead of using the mouse to select the command from a menu.

Creating Your First Document

It is now time to put you to work so you can learn this wonderful program. In this chapter, you'll type a sample letter to experiment with. Remember, go at your own pace. Get the words onscreen so you can practice making changes. Once you've finished typing, you'll see how to move the cursor around your document, save it for future use, close the document, and exit from Word for Windows.

Definition of a Document or File

In the first chapter, you saw the word *document* used frequently to refer to the collected words you type, as well as what you save on your disk. Another word often used is *file*. *File* and *document* are interchangeable terms. You might, for example, hear friends say they need to copy a file to their floppy disk, but that they're busy working on a document that is important to this afternoon's meeting. Let's start working on *your* first document.

Typing a Sample Letter

To start creating a sample letter, type in today's date, then press the ENTER key twice. This pushes the cursor two lines beneath the date. Before continuing with the letter, here are a few Word for Windows features that you should know about.

ENTER Key

The ENTER key is used to end a paragraph, whether it is several lines long or only part of one line.

BACKSPACE Key

Even if you are a pretty good typist, chances are you might make an error while typing this letter. If you make a mistake, use the BACKSPACE key to erase the character immediately to the left of the cursor.

Wordwrap

When you get to the end of the first line of the letter, you do not need to press ENTER to move the cursor to the next line—Word for Windows does it for you. This feature is called *wordwrap*. The program automatically determines how many words will fit on a line and pushes the next word to the following line.

Continuing the Sample Letter

Now you're ready to resume typing the sample letter. Following are the opening greeting and the first two paragraphs of the letter, which will be the basis for the exercises in this chapter and in chapters to follow. Type the opening and press ENTER twice to start a new paragraph and move the cursor down an extra line. Then type the two paragraphs, pressing ENTER once at the end of each paragraph.

> Dear Freda:
>
> I received a wonderful travel brochure describing an exciting rafting trip that I'm sure we would both enjoy. This would be a great opportunity for us to try a new adventure. Here's a blurb outlining the trip for the Kings River in California:
> Spanish explorers first came across the Kings River on January 6, 1805. Since January 6 is the feast of the Epiphany which celebrates the arrival of the three kings in Bethlehem, the river was named "El Rio de los Santo Reyes"—River of the Holy Kings. Originating in Sequoia/Kings Canyon National Park, the Kings River is the largest river in the Sierras. During spring runoff (late April through mid-June), the Kings provides some of the most exciting whitewater in the state.

Cursor Movement

After typing the preceding example, you might need to move the cursor to a previous part of the document to make some changes or corrections to your text. There are several ways to get you where you want to go.

Arrow Keys

The arrow keys are usually located between the bottom right of the keyboard and the numeric keypad.

- The UP ARROW key moves your cursor up one line at a time.

- The DOWN ARROW key moves your cursor down one line at a time.

- The LEFT ARROW and RIGHT ARROW keys move the cursor left and right one character at a time, respectively.

Using the Mouse

If you choose to use the mouse, position the mouse pointer where you want the cursor to be and click once. It is important that you click at the new location. You'll know it's there because the cursor flashes at the new location. This method might be a little difficult at first, since you have to position the mouse pointer exactly where you want the cursor to appear.

Keypad Arrow Keys

You can use the arrow keys on the numeric keypad as long as the NUM LOCK key is off. When NUM LOCK is on, you can use the numbers written on the keys.

If you look at the status bar (at the bottom of the screen) and "NUM" appears, then NUM LOCK is on, and pressing one of the keypad keys produces a number on the screen at the cursor position. To use the keypad keys as directional keys, press the NUM LOCK key to make the "NUM" message disappear from the status bar.

END and HOME Keys

The END key is a quick way to move the cursor to the end of the current line. It's much faster than holding down the RIGHT ARROW key until the cursor reaches the end of the line.

Similarly, the HOME key moves the cursor to the beginning of the current line.

PAGE UP and PAGE DOWN Keys

The PAGE UP key moves the cursor up one screen at a time, and the PAGE DOWN key moves the cursor down one screen at a time. These keys are useful when your document is longer than what is visible on one screen.

Bigger Jumps

To move to the *end* of the document, press CTRL-END. To go to the *beginning* of the document, press CTRL-HOME. (Remember: hold down the CTRL key, then press HOME or END.)

To go to a specific page, press F5, type in the page you want, then press ENTER.

Using the Scroll Bars

The scroll bars allow you to view different areas of the file.

Tip: If you use the scroll bars to see a different part of the document, be aware that, although you are viewing a different part of the file, your cursor is still back at the original location. If you want to move the cursor to where you have scrolled, click the mouse at that new location. If you start typing without first clicking, Word for Windows thinks you are inserting text back at the cursor, and your screen returns to the cursor location.

Here are some instructions for using the scroll bar to view different portions of a document. You use the mouse, the vertical scroll bar, and the scroll box.

- Click the up or down arrow to move the viewing area up or down one line at a time.
- Click the vertical scroll bar above or below the scroll box to move the viewing area up or down one screen at a time.
- Drag (click and hold) the scroll box up or down and then release the mouse to move the viewing area up or down.

If you drag the scroll box halfway down the scroll bar and release the mouse, the *top line* of the viewing area is halfway down your file. This type of viewing milestone works regardless of file length. For example, if your file is 100 pages, dragging the scroll box halfway down the scroll bar and releasing your mouse changes your view to approximately page 50.

Remember: If you change the viewing area and want to likewise move the cursor, click at the desired position on the new screen.

Dialog Boxes

A *dialog box* is a box that appears when certain commands are selected. Many commands you will use while working on your document cause a dialog box to appear. Before you continue with your document, this would be a good time to take a look at how to use dialog boxes.

The different items in a dialog box allow you to change the settings or options for that particular command, as demonstrated in the Page Setup dialog box.

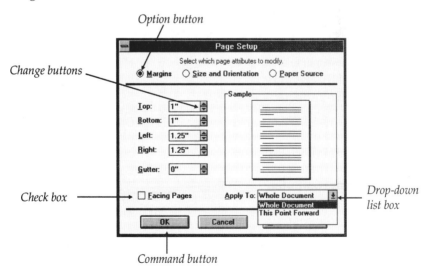

Option button

Change buttons

Check box

Drop-down list box

Command button

When you're satisfied with the changes you've made in a dialog box, click the OK command button. A *command button* is labeled with the function it performs. Most dialog boxes have a Cancel command button to allow exiting the dialog box without saving any changes.

Some dialog boxes contain a *drop-down list box*. The default setting is displayed within the box. To see the other choices available, click the arrow at the end of the box. To change to one of the other choices, click the desired option.

Change buttons look like the minimize and maximize/restore buttons for your program: two small triangles pointing up and down. If the up or down arrow is clicked, the value in the adjacent box increases or decreases, respectively.

Check boxes are squares that toggle a feature on or off. If the box is empty, the feature is off. To turn the feature on, click the box. An "x" appears in the box. To turn the feature off, click the box, and the "x" goes away.

Option buttons look like circles. They have a black dot in the middle of the circle if that option is selected. If the option is not selected, then the circle is empty. Often, selecting one button will deselect other option buttons.

Saving the Document

After typing for a while, it is a good idea to save your work. If you want to go do something else and need to turn off the computer, you must save your document if you want to be able to access it again. As mentioned in Chapter 1, your document is only temporarily stored in the RAM of your computer. Any text that is not saved to a disk is lost once the computer is turned off.

Why You Should Save Your Files

A power failure that turns the computer off can cause you to lose what you have typed, unless you have named and saved your document before-hand.

A good milestone for saving your work is once every 3 to 4 paragraphs, or every 15 minutes, whichever comes first. (This seems to become really easy to remember after the first time text is accidentally lost.)

To save your document, open the File menu and select Save As. Notice the ellipsis (...) after Save As. The ellipsis following any menu command indicates that a dialog box will appear if the command is chosen.

The Save As dialog box appears on your screen. The cursor is blinking in a box beneath File Name.

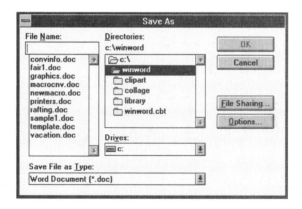

Tip: If you accidentally choose the wrong command, virtually all Word for Windows dialog boxes contain a Cancel button that allows you to return to the document.

Type rafting in the box and click OK. The hourglass appears briefly to let you know that the document is being saved. At the top of your screen, the word *Document1* is replaced with *RAFTING.DOC*. Congratulations! You've saved your first Word for Windows document. If you were to lose computer power now, you would not have to type the letter all over again.

Naming Files

There are certain rules and regulations that apply to naming files. The following is a helpful guide for naming your documents.

Character Restrictions

DOS requires that you use only specific characters when naming your documents. You cannot use spaces or any of the following characters:

/ \ * ? | ^ & < > ; : , .

Word for Windows will prevent you from including these characters in filenames.

Name Length Limitations

A filename can be up to eight characters long. This is the upper limit that DOS, and therefore Word for Windows, allows.

Word for Windows automatically adds the file extension .DOC to the end of each filename. Since spaces are not allowed, a file called MY MEMO could be named MY_MEMO or MY-MEMO, and the official name of this file becomes MY_MEMO.DOC or MY-MEMO.DOC. If you try to name a file PROJECTIONS FOR NEXT YEAR, the file is saved as PROJECTI.DOC, the first eight characters you typed.

Tip: Even though Word for Windows automatically adds the file extension .DOC, any other allowed characters (up to three) can be used. Just type in the full filename that you want, including the extension. This can be useful in grouping the files by some common extension.

If you try to assign a name that has already been taken to a file, Word for Windows offers a message asking whether you would like to replace the existing file with the active document.

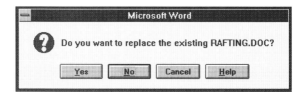

If you choose Yes, the file that previously had the name goes to computer heaven; it no longer exists. The file on the screen now has that filename.

If you choose No, Word for Windows returns to the Save As dialog box to allow you to type in another name.

If you choose Cancel, Word for Windows returns to the document.

Directory Organization

Word for Windows saves a file in the same subdirectory as the program, usually WINWORD. In the Save As dialog box shown earlier, WINWORD was the default directory. A *directory* or *subdirectory* (the terms are used interchangeably) is a placeholder for a group of files. Directories are used to group similar items or files that have some relationship to one another. You might want to group all your letters concerning a particular client in one directory so it will be easier to locate these similar letters.

If you want to create other directories, refer to your Windows documentation concerning the File Manager and creating directories.

Closing the Active Document

Since you have saved RAFTING.DOC to the hard disk, you can now close the file. *Closing* the file removes, or clears, the file from the screen. The text is not lost because it has already been saved. Chapter 3 will show you how to open an existing file after it has been closed. Closing the file does not prevent you from creating another file or opening another file. Closing the file also does not exit you from Word for Windows.

For practice, choose Close from the File menu. If you haven't made any alterations since the last save, RAFTING.DOC will disappear from the screen.

If you have made a change, even pressing the spacebar, a dialog box appears, asking if you want to save the changes. If you did correct some errors, click Yes.

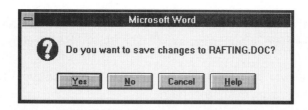

Because there is no active document now, some of the menus have disappeared from the menu bar. Don't worry. It only means that at this point, with no files open, you can't perform certain commands until you have a new document window open.

Quitting Word for Windows and Windows

To leave the Word for Windows program, select Exit from the File menu. To quit Microsoft Windows:

1. Click the Program Manager program group, and press ENTER.

2. Using your mouse, choose Exit Windows from the File menu.

3. Click OK. The computer returns to the DOS prompt.

What Do They Mean By...?

ENTER Key   The key used to end a paragraph and to insert blank lines between paragraphs.

Cursor   A marker that indicates where text will be inserted when you type.

Wordwrap   A feature that allows the cursor to move to the next line of text automatically while you are typing.

Arrow Keys   The keyboard keys that move the cursor left, right, up, and down.

Save   A command to store your text for future review and editing.

File   A body of text that is typed on a computer and saved for future use.

Document   Another name for a file.

Close   A command that removes, or clears, a window from the screen. If the document you were working on in the window hasn't been saved, Word for Windows will ask you if you want to save or discard the file.

Quit   A command used to leave an application. When you quit from Word for Windows, you are returned to Windows' Program Manager.

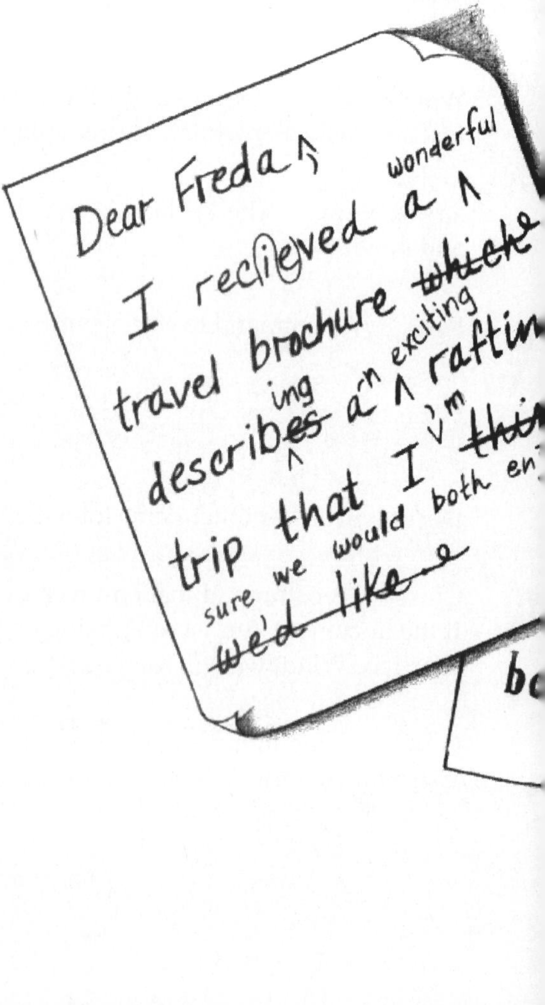

Dear Freda ⌃,
I reci⟨e⟩ved a ⌃wonderful
travel brochure ~~which~~
describes ⌃ing a⌃n ⌃exciting raftin
trip that I ⌃'m ~~thi~~
sure we would both en
~~we'd like~~

Editing and Printing Your Document

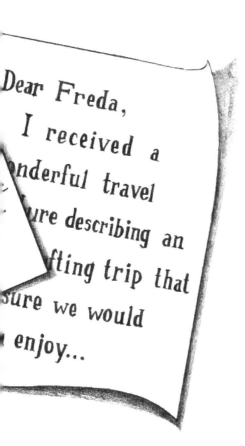

Dear Freda,
I received a
nderful travel
re describing an
ting trip that
ure we would
enjoy...

After creating a document, it is a smart idea to go back and review it before handing it over to a reader. As you review it, you might decide that the wording needs to be modified. Adding text, deleting text, and adding blank lines are some of the features described by the word *editing*.

Once you are satisfied with the changes, the revised file needs to be saved again. You want to re-save the file to ensure that what is on the hard disk is the most up-to-date version. Another option is to keep your original file intact and save the revisions to a new file.

After re-saving the file, you can preview the file on the screen before sending it to the printer.

Opening an Existing Document

You might want to open an existing file so you can review it, make any necessary changes, save the changes, and print it. If you are not in Windows now, start it up, and then load Word for Windows. Refer to Chapter 1 for a review of these steps.

To retrieve, or open, a document, select Open from the File menu. The Open dialog box appears.

On the left side beneath the label File Name is a box showing an alphabetical list of existing files in your WINWORD directory. (The list of files on your screen may be different than what is shown in this book.) Double-click RAFTING.DOC to open the document.

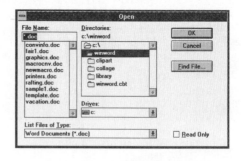

Tip: Alternatively, you can click RAFTING.DOC once, then click OK to open the file.

Modifying the Document

Sometimes you might need to change the wording of your document, or add or delete text. You might also want to insert blank lines to separate paragraphs.

Adding Text

In the letter on your screen, add a sentence to the second paragraph. Move your cursor to just before the word *Originating* in the sentence that begins, "Originating in Sequoia/Kings Canyon National Park...." (This is the second to last sentence.) Press the SPACEBAR once and then type the following:

We guarantee that you will feel like "royalty," on this, our most popular river.

Notice that Word for Windows inserts the new words and pushes the text that follows the cursor further down the page.

Adding Blank Lines

To make the letter easier to read, insert a blank line between the two paragraphs. Position the cursor at the end of the first paragraph, just after the colon at the end of the word *California*. Press ENTER once. As when you insert text, the ENTER key pushes all text following the cursor down the page.

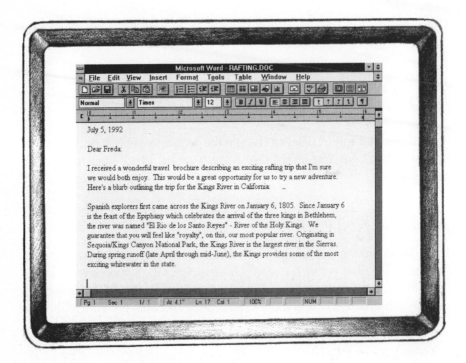

Deleting Text

If you want to delete text from your letter, you can use the DEL (Delete) key. This key removes one character at a time to the *right* of the cursor.

Position the cursor just before the words *for us* in the first paragraph of the sample letter and press the DEL key. The letter "f" disappears. Press the DEL key five more times to delete the words *for us.*

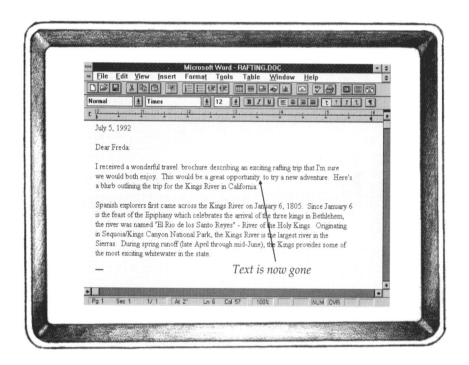

Text is now gone

Tip: The BACKSPACE *key can also be used to delete text. On many keyboards, it is labeled with a left-pointing arrow. The* BACKSPACE *key removes the character just to the left of the cursor. An easy way to differentiate between* BACKSPACE *and* DEL *is that the* BACKSPACE *arrow points in the direction (to the left) that characters are removed.*

Replacing Text Using the INS Key

As you have seen, when you type in new text, the existing text moves to make room for the new words. This is called insert mode. By pressing the INS (Insert) key, you can

toggle back and forth between insert mode and overtype mode. In overtype mode, new text types over, or replaces, the old text. When you are in overtype mode, "OVR" appears on the status bar at the bottom of the screen.

Try this example to see how the INS key works:

Overtype mode

1. Position the cursor to the left of the name Freda at the top of the letter.

2. Press the INS key. You should now be in overtype mode.

3. Type **Grace**. The name Freda is replaced by Grace.

4. To return to the name Freda, position the cursor to the left of the "G" in *Grace*, then type **Freda**.

To go back to insert mode, press INS again. Until you're comfortable using Word for Windows, it is best to stay in insert mode so you don't accidentally delete text.

Continuing the Letter

Now let's add another paragraph to the sample letter. Move the cursor so it is positioned on the line below the last paragraph. Press ENTER to add a blank line. Here is the next paragraph of the letter for you to type:

```
Unlike most other rivers where flows of 10,000 cubic
feet per second or more usually mean trip cancellation,
the Kings just gets more exciting and is still runnable.
From late June until season end (depending on the amount
of spring runoff), the Kings slowly calms to a frisky
class 3 run, with crystal clear water, wonderful
swimming, great fishing and excellent rapids.
```

Saving Changes

After several editing revisions, you probably want to save the changes to your hard disk so that they aren't lost in the case of a power failure. When you save changes, the previously saved version of the file is deleted from the hard disk. To save the letter onscreen, choose Save from the File menu.

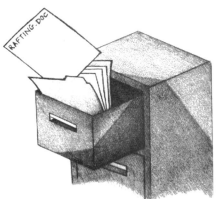

The Save command in Word for Windows does not open a dialog box if you're saving changes to a named file. In this case, you are saving an updated version of RAFTING.DOC, therefore the old RAFTING.DOC goes to computer heaven; it no longer exists.

Printing the Document

Printing a file produces a copy of the file on paper, allowing you to give your document to someone else to read. You could ask someone to sit at your screen and read the file, but printing a copy is probably an easier way to allow others

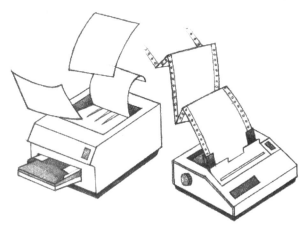

to see what you have written. To print a file, choose Print from the File menu.

The Print Command

When you select the Print command, the Print dialog box appears. In the dialog box, the first line, labeled Printer, indicates the name of the printer and the name of the port on the computer that the printer is connected to.

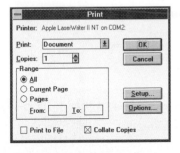

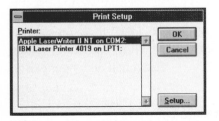

If the printer name does not appear here, click the Setup button. The Print Setup dialog box opens. Click the correct name of your printer and port, then click OK to return to the Print dialog box.

Note: If your printer is not listed in the Print Setup dialog box, click Cancel to return to the Print dialog box. Click Cancel again to return to the document. You will need to use Windows' Print Manager to install your printer. Refer to your Windows documentation for these steps.

The next box in the Print dialog box is labeled Print. The word *Document* in this box indicates that the document text is going to be printed, as opposed to other attributes of the file. To see the other document attributes, click the down arrow to the right of the box. A drop-down list appears showing the other possible items.

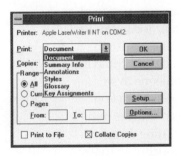

Click the arrow again to make the list disappear. For further information on the other items, refer to the Word for Windows user's guide.

The Copies box allows you to specify how many copies of the file you want printed. By clicking the up and down change buttons, you set the number of copies to print.

Tip: You can also drag the mouse over the copy number to select it, then type the number of copies.

The Range box gives you the option to print the entire file, the current page (the page your cursor is on when you choose the Print command), or a range of pages, such as page 8 to page 15. To change the range, click the From box and type in the beginning page number. Then click the To box and type the ending page number.

Note: If you leave the To box blank, Word for Windows prints pages starting at the From page to the end of the file.

The Collate Copies check box is useful when you choose to print more than one copy of a multipage file. For example, if you print three copies of a five-page file with Collate Copies off, Word for Windows prints three copies of page one, then three copies of page two, and so on. With Collate Copies selected, collating of the three copies is done for you.

When you have made your choices, click OK, and RAFTING.DOC should print on paper.

Print Preview

Before printing a document, it can be helpful to see onscreen what the printed copy will look like. Word for Windows has a command called Print Preview that gives you a bird's-eye view of your file before sending the file to the printer. This allows you to verify that everything you want in the file is there. If your document is a multiple-page file, you can page through it in Print Preview.

Note: You cannot edit the text while in Print Preview.

Choose Print Preview from the File menu. Your screen should appear similar to the following.

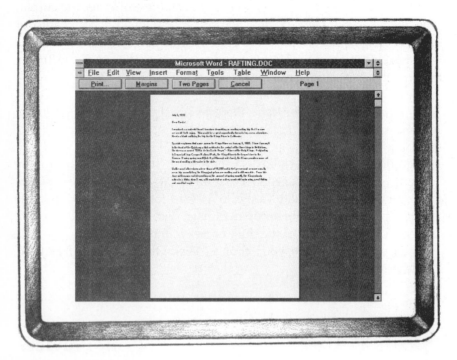

There are four buttons on the Print Preview window:

- Print
- Margins
- Two Pages
- Cancel

The Print button opens the same dialog box you see when you choose the Print command.

The Margins button displays the current top, bottom, left, and right margins of the file. If you adjust the margins, the changes are made for each page of the file.

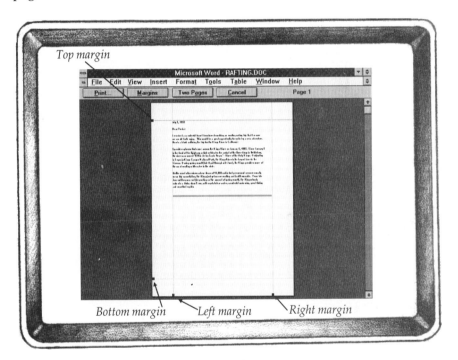

To adjust the left and right margins of RAFTING.DOC:

1. Click the Margins button at the top of the Print Preview window.

2. Position the mouse pointer on the black box at the bottom of the vertical gray line representing the left margin.

3. When the pointer turns into a crosshair icon (it looks like a plus (+) sign), press and hold the mouse button.

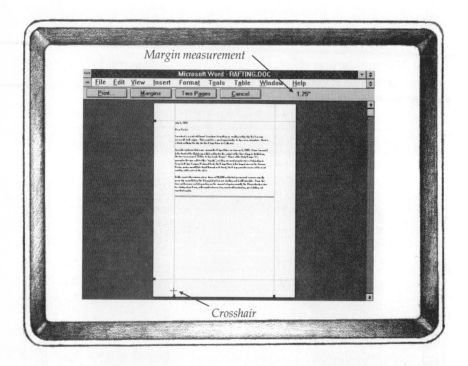

You will notice a measurement in inches appear in the upper-right corner of the screen. (The page number temporarily changes to the inch measurement.)

4. Drag the mouse to the right until the number changes to 1.5", then release the mouse.

5. Change the right margin in the same way. Position the mouse pointer on the black box at the bottom of the vertical gray line representing the right margin, but drag the mouse to the left. Increase its size to 1.5 inches.

6. To have the new margins take effect, click the Margins button, press ENTER, or click anywhere outside the page.

7. Return the margins to their original measurements by dragging the left and the right margins back to 1.25 inches.

8. Click the Margin button to reset the margins.

9. Click the Close button.

The Two Pages button allows you to preview two pages at a time. If you have a one-page document, the right-hand page is blank. To return to single-page preview, click the button that now reads One Page. When you click the One Page or Two Pages button, the Cancel button changes to Close. The Cancel or Close button returns you to the document.

Saving a Copy

There may be occasions when you want to keep your original document unchanged while modifying a copy of the file. Word for Windows uses the Save As command to do this. You also used Save As to name the file the first time you saved it.

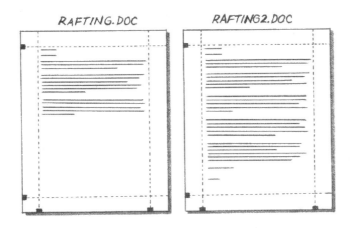

Before you save the letter, position the cursor after the last line of text in RAFTING.DOC and type the following text:

> Trips are run out of our beautiful 5 acre base camp right on the
> banks of the river. Our full time chef will tantalize you with
> exquisite river cuisine, and our sandy riverfront campsites are
> the finest anywhere. Picnic tables, campsite barbecues, and a
> volleyball court are provided for your convenience. Arrive the
> evening before your trip, set up your campsite, and relax on the
> banks of the Kings River.
>
> Does this sound like a great way to spend a couple of days or
> what? I called last week and they have some openings at the end
> of August. Let's go for it, Freda! Call me and let me know what
> you think.
>
> Speak to you soon,
>
> Cathy

After you finish typing the letter, choose Save As from the File menu. The Save As dialog box appears. Beneath File Name, the current document name RAFTING.DOC is highlighted. Type **rafting2**, which replaces RAFTING.DOC in the File Name box. Click OK, and now the active document is RAFTING2.DOC. The original RAFTING.DOC is still saved, with just the first three paragraphs.

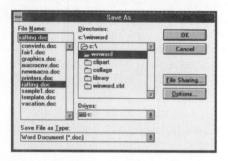

As a reminder, use Save As:

- When saving a file for the first time

- When adding changes to an existing file, if you want to keep the original file intact and save the changed file under another name

Use Save:

- When adding changes to an existing file, if you want to overwrite the existing file

What Do They Mean By...?

BACKSPACE **Key**   A key, frequently labeled with a left-pointing arrow, that deletes one character to the left of the cursor.

DEL **Key**   A key that deletes one character to the right of the cursor.

Print Preview   A command to see a bird's-eye view of your document onscreen before printing. You cannot edit text while in Print Preview mode.

Save As   A command that allows you to save a file under a different filename, keeping the original file intact.

Handling
Blocks of Text

If you want to modify parts of your document in Word for Windows, you need to tell the program which words should be changed. This is done by selecting, or highlighting, the words. Once they are selected, you can perform many commands on the highlighted block of words. For example, if you want to make the headline of a report stand out by bolding the text, you can select the text and then issue the bold command. (Bolding and other enhancements are covered in Chapter 7.) There is no need to delete, then retype with the bold feature turned on.

For the exercises in this chapter, you will use the RAFTING2.DOC file you created in Chapter 3. Choose Open from the File menu and double-click RAFTING2.DOC to open this file.

Selecting Text

There are various methods available to highlight blocks of text. You can select from a single character up to the entire file.

Selecting a Character or Characters

There are two methods to select a single character or small group of characters. One method uses the mouse and the other involves the keyboard.

Dear Freda,

To use the mouse method, you drag the mouse pointer over the letters. If you begin with the pointer to the left of the characters, hold down the mouse button and drag to the right. If your pointer is to the right of the characters, drag the mouse to the left.

Tip: If you select the wrong characters, click an area of the screen away from the highlighted block. This action unselects the block so you can try again.

To use the keyboard, position the cursor so it is to one side of the desired character. Hold down SHIFT and press the LEFT ARROW or RIGHT ARROW key (depending on which side of the character your cursor is sitting). If you don't hold down the SHIFT key, you are just moving the cursor.

Tip: If you select the wrong characters, remove your finger from the SHIFT *key and press one of the arrow keys. This action unselects the block and you can try again.*

Another keyboard method also begins by positioning the cursor to one side of the desired character. Then press F8 and press the LEFT ARROW or RIGHT ARROW key (depending on which side of the character your cursor is sitting).

Tip: When using the second keyboard method, if you select the wrong characters, press ESC *once, then press an arrow key to unselect the characters.*

There is no right or wrong way to highlight a character. If you are new to using the mouse, try a keyboard method until mouse movement feels more natural.

For practice, highlight the date in the sample letter and change it to two days ago.

Selecting a Word

Dear Freda,

There are four ways to select a word:

- Double-click the word.
- Use the mouse to drag across the entire word.
- Hold down the CTRL and SHIFT keys together (use your left hand to hold down both keys) and press the LEFT ARROW or RIGHT ARROW key.
- Position the cursor anywhere within the word and press F8 twice. If you select the wrong word, press ESC and press an arrow key to unselect the word.

Selecting a Sentence

> Dear Freda:
>
> I received a wonderful travel brochure describing an exciting rafting trip that I'm sure we would both enjoy. This would be a great opportunity to try a new adventure. Here's a blurb outlining the trip for the Kings River in California:

To select an entire sentence, you have three options:

- Drag the mouse pointer across the entire sentence.
- Position the mouse pointer anywhere within the sentence. Hold down the CTRL key, then click the mouse once.
- Position the cursor anywhere within the sentence. Press F8 three times. If you select the wrong sentence, press ESC and then press an arrow key to unselect the sentence.

Tip: The second and third methods work well unless your sentence contains a decimal point or period in the text. For example, in the sentences, "I will send you $44.95 next week" and "The report to Mr. Gimpel will be finished on Monday," Word for Windows highlights only up to the period or decimal point.

Selecting a Line of Text

> Spanish explorers first came across the Kings River on January 6, 1805. Since January 6 is the feast of the Epiphany which celebrates the arrival of the three kings in Bethlehem, the river was named "El Rio de los Santo Reyes" - River of the Holy Kings. We guarantee that you will feel like "royalty", on this, our most popular river. Originating in Sequoia/Kings Canyon National Park, the Kings River is the largest river in the Sierras. During spring runoff (late April through mid-June), the Kings provides some of the most exciting whitewater in the state.

To select a line of text:

Position the mouse pointer to the far left of the line to be selected (as mentioned in Chapter 1, the extreme left side of a document is called the selection area). You know you are in the correct position when the mouse pointer changes from an I-beam to an arrow pointing up and to the right.

Click the mouse once, and the entire line of text is highlighted.

Selecting a Paragraph

> Dear Freda:
>
> I received a wonderful travel brochure describing an exciting rafting trip that I'm sure we would both enjoy. This would be a great opportunity to try a new adventure. Here's a blurb outlining the trip for the Kings River in California:

To select a paragraph, you have these options:

- Position the mouse pointer in the selection area next to the desired paragraph, then double-click.

- Move the cursor so it is blinking to the left of the first character of the paragraph. Hold down the CTRL and SHIFT keys, then press the DOWN ARROW key.

- Position the cursor anywhere within the paragraph. Press F8 four times. If you select the wrong paragraph, press ESC and press an arrow key to unselect the paragraph.

Selecting a Block

> Dear Freda:
>
> I received a wonderful travel brochure describing an exciting rafting trip that I'm sure we would both enjoy. This would be a great opportunity to try a new adventure. Here's a blurb outlining the trip for the Kings River in California:
>
> Spanish explorers first came across the Kings River on January 6, 1805. Since January 6 is the feast of the Epiphany which celebrates the arrival of the three kings in Bethlehem, the river was named "El Rio de los Santo Reyes" - River of the Holy Kings. We guarantee that you will feel like "royalty", on this, our most popular river. Originating in Sequoia/Kings Canyon National Park, the Kings River is the largest river in the Sierras. During spring runoff (late April through mid-June), the Kings provides some of the most exciting whitewater in the state.

In some situations, you may need to select a block of text that is of any size. There are two methods available.

- Click at the beginning of the block and drag the mouse to the end of the block.

- Click at the beginning of the block, and then hold down the SHIFT key. Position the mouse pointer at the end of the block and click again.

Tip: If a block is already highlighted, you can adjust the amount of selected text by pressing the SHIFT key and clicking after the last desired character.

Selecting Multiple Paragraphs

To select multiple paragraphs, position the mouse pointer in the selection area next to the first line of the first paragraph, then hold down the mouse button and drag straight down to the end of the last paragraph.

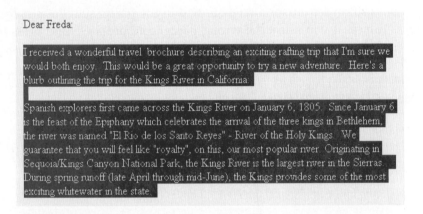

Tip: You can also use the second method for selecting a block mentioned in the section "Selecting a Block." This method is preferable if the amount of text you need to select is more than what is visible on the screen. You can position the cursor at the beginning of the block and click the down arrow in the vertical scroll bar to

view further down the file. Then, hold down the SHIFT *key and click at the end of the block.*

Selecting the Entire Document

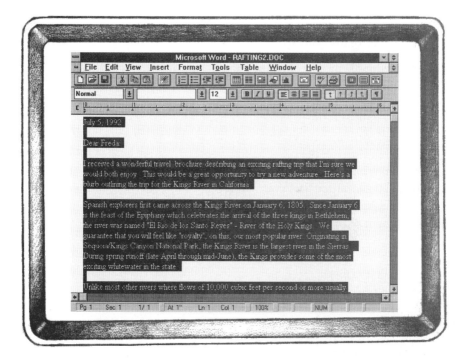

There are two methods to select the entire file. These methods work regardless of the page you are currently working on.

- Position the mouse pointer in the selection area and hold down the CTRL key. Click once.

- Hold down the CTRL key and press the 5 key on the numeric keypad.

Remember that once any block is selected, you can perform many commands on that block. For example, you can delete the block, make it bold or double-spaced, or change the type style or font size. Bolding text, changing fonts, and changing point sizes are covered in Chapter 7, and double spacing text is discussed in Chapter 8. Deleting a block is covered in the next practice example in this chapter.

For practice, try highlighting the following blocks of text in the sample letter:

- The entire line that contains the date
- The first paragraph
- The first sentence of the second paragraph
- The "D" in *Dear Freda*
- The name Freda
- The entire letter

Now let's highlight and delete a sentence. Highlight the sentence that begins, "We guarantee that you will feel...," in the second paragraph. Press DEL and the sentence disappears. Choose Save from the File menu to save the document with this change.

Moving Text

There might come a time when you need to move text from one place to another within your file. You could delete it from the original location and then retype it in the new place, but this option would probably make you

crazy after the fifth or sixth time. That's why Word for Windows comes to your rescue with a feature called Cut, located on the Edit menu.

What Is Cut and Paste?

If you have ever used a pair of scissors to remove an article from a newspaper or magazine, you have physically cut the text. If you put the article on a piece of paper, you used tape or glue to paste it in its new location. With Word for Windows, cutting and pasting is all done electronically on the screen.

Both the Cut and Paste commands are on the Edit menu.

The Cut command temporarily removes a highlighted block from the screen. Don't worry, the words are not lost. The Clipboard holds the text until you use the Paste command to insert the text somewhere. The *Clipboard* is an electronic storage area that temporarily holds selected text or graphics when you choose the Cut or Copy command. Items stay on the Clipboard until the next time you use the Cut or Copy command.

Edit	
Can't Undo	Ctrl+Z
Can't Repeat	F4
Cut	Ctrl+X
Copy	Ctrl+C
Paste	Ctrl+V
Paste Special...	
Select All	Ctrl+NumPad 5
Find...	
Replace...	
Go To...	F5
Glossary...	
Links...	
Object...	

Copying Text

The Copy command, also on the Edit menu, allows you to place a duplicate of the selected block on the Clipboard. The original text or graphics are not removed from the screen.

When you move the cursor to a new location and choose Paste, the contents of the Clipboard are placed at the cursor position.

How to Cut or Copy and Paste

There are four steps to perform a cut or copy and paste:

1. Highlight the text. Use any of the methods mentioned previously for selecting a block of text.

2. Choose either Cut or Copy from the Edit menu.

3. Move the cursor to the desired location.

4. Choose Paste from the Edit menu.

Drag-and-Drop

Drag-and-drop allows you to quickly move selected items to a new location. This method is similar to the Cut and Paste command combination, except it does not move items to the Clipboard.

This feature needs to be activated to work. To activate Drag-and-drop:

1. Choose Options from the Tools menu.

2. In the Category column, click the General icon.

3. If the check box next to Drag-and-drop Text Editing contains an "x", the feature is active. If the feature is inactive, click the check box now to turn on the feature.

4. Click OK to return to the document screen.

Drag-and-drop option

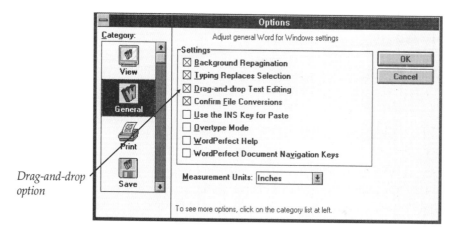

To use Drag-and-drop:

1. Highlight the text.

2. Place the mouse pointer within the block.

3. Hold down the left mouse button. The mouse pointer should now be a little gray square and a gray arrow.

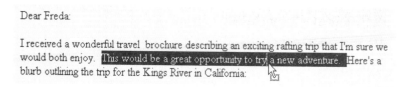

4. Drag the mouse to a new location. The gray cursor indicates where the block is to be dropped. It appears only when using Drag-and-drop.

> Dear Freda:
>
> I received a wonderful travel brochure describing an exciting rafting trip that I'm sure we would both enjoy. This would be a great opportunity to try a new adventure. Here's a blurb outlining the trip for the Kings River in California.

5. Release the mouse button. The text has been moved to the new location.

> Dear Freda:
>
> I received a wonderful travel brochure describing an exciting rafting trip that I'm sure we would both enjoy. Here's a blurb outlining the trip for the Kings River in California. This would be a great opportunity to try a new adventure.

Drag-and-drop is most practical if what you have to move, and where you are moving it to, are both visible on the screen. You need to keep your finger pressing down the mouse button until the text is in the new location. If you have to move it too far, you might release the button and drop the text in the wrong place. If you need to move text from one page to another, the Cut and Paste commands are easier to use. Experiment for yourself and see what works best for you.

For practice, let's move some parts of the letter around:

1. Highlight the sentence in the second paragraph that begins "Originating in Sequoia/Kings Canyon...." Refer to the earlier section, "Selecting a Sentence," for instructions.

2. Choose Cut from the Edit menu.

3. Move the cursor after the last sentence of the same paragraph. Press SPACEBAR so there will be a space before the incoming sentence.

4. Choose Paste from the Edit menu.

5. Highlight the date at the top of the letter.

6. Choose Copy from the Edit menu.

7. Move the cursor to the line above "Speak to you soon," located at the end of the letter.

8. Choose Paste from the Edit menu.

Undo

Assume the text you just pasted is not in the correct place. Instead of re-highlighting it and choosing Cut again, you can choose Undo from the Edit menu. The *Undo* command allows you to reverse your last action.

Depending on your last action, the Undo message in the menu changes. For example, if you deleted a block of text and realized it was the wrong block, immediately choose Undo Typing, and the text will return to the screen. If you make a block bold, the command reads Undo Formatting to return the block to normal text.

Edit	
Undo Paste	Ctrl+Z
Repeat Paste	F4
Cut	Ctrl+X
Copy	Ctrl+C
Paste	Ctrl+V
Paste Special...	
Select All	Ctrl+NumPad 5
Find...	
Replace...	
Go To...	F5
Glossary...	
Links...	
Object...	

Tip: The Undo feature in Word for Windows reverses only the last action. Therefore, if you perform Cut and then Paste, Undo Paste reverses only the Paste, not the Cut. If you then want to put the text back where it was, place the cursor where you wish to reinsert the text and choose Paste.

After you choose Undo, the Undo option changes to Undo Undo. If you realize that you did want to keep your original action, choose this command.

Repeat

Depending on the last action, Word for Windows might show a Repeat command under the Undo command. If you want to perform that action again, you can select Repeat from the Edit menu.

For example, if you make a block of text bold, the Edit menu shows Undo Formatting and Repeat Formatting. The Repeat command will generally be available when changing character or paragraph formats.

For practice:

1. Highlight the words *travel brochure* in the first paragraph.
2. Press DEL to remove the text.
3. Choose Undo from the Edit menu to bring the text back.

For more practice:

1. Highlight the last sentence of the first paragraph.
2. Choose Cut from the Edit menu.
3. Choose Undo Cut from the Edit menu.
4. Choose Undo Undo from the Edit menu.
5. Choose Undo Cut from the Edit menu.

Edit	
Undo Formatting	Ctrl+Z
Repeat Formatting	F4
Cut	Ctrl+X
Copy	Ctrl+C
Paste	Ctrl+V
Paste Special...	
Select All	Ctrl+NumPad 5
Find...	
Replace...	
Go To...	F5
Glossary...	
Links...	
Object...	

To finish, choose Close from the File menu and click No to not save the changes. Choosing not to save changes will keep the last saved version of RAFTING2.DOC as it was before you practiced Cut and Paste.

What Do They Mean By...?

Block of Text   Any group of characters that is temporarily highlighted on the screen.

Clipboard   A temporary holding area for text that has been cut or copied. It holds only one block at a time. The next time Cut or Copy is used, the item that was on the Clipboard is replaced by the new Cut or Copy text.

Copy   A command that puts a duplicate of a block of text onto the Clipboard. The text also stays at its original location.

Cut   A command that removes a block of text from the screen onto the Clipboard. Usually the text is to be moved to another location within the file.

Undo   A command that reverses your last action.

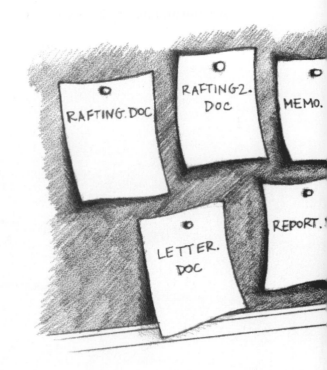

Working with Multiple Documents

So far, you have worked with RAFTING.DOC and have created RAFT-ING2.DOC by using the Save As command. After using Save As, RAFT-ING.DOC disappeared from the screen, and RAFTING2.DOC became the active file. What if you wanted to work with *both* files and move back and forth between them? It's possible with Word for Windows.

Many word processors allow you to work with only one file at a time, which means you must close one file before opening another or creating a new file. There may come a time, however, when you need to copy (or cut) a part of one file and place it into a different file.

Amazingly enough, Word for Windows allows up to *nine* open documents at a time, each in its own separate window. There can be only one active document at any time, however. The other documents are in inactive windows, usually behind the active document.

Imagine a deck with nine cards. Any of the cards can be brought to the top of the deck. In Word for Windows, the top card is the *active window*. Nine files might be a little much for anyone to keep track of, but having two or three open files can be useful, so you can copy text easily from one to another.

This chapter shows you how to split the window of one document so you can see different parts of it at the same time. You will also learn how to view more than one document onscreen simultaneously, and you will practice copying and pasting between windows.

Splitting the Window of One Document

A useful Word for Windows feature splits the window of the active document. *Splitting* the window allows you to see two parts of the same document. Word for Windows calls each part a window *pane*.

For example, to verify that topics mentioned on page one are covered on page six, you could move to page six, verify that the information is there, and then return to page one. By splitting the screen, it is possible to see page one at the top of the screen and page six at the bottom, simultaneously.

To practice splitting a window, retrieve RAFTING2.DOC (choose Open from the File menu). Then perform the following steps:

1. Notice the small black bar just above the up arrow in the vertical scroll bar. This bar is called the *split screen bar*.

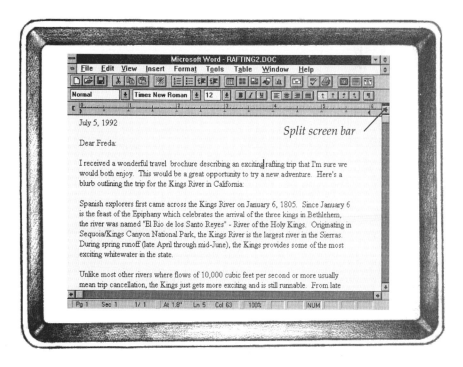

2. Position the mouse pointer on the split screen bar. You'll know you are in the correct position when the mouse pointer changes to a black bar with arrows pointing up and down from the bar.

←*Position the pointer here*

3. Hold down the mouse button and drag approximately halfway down the vertical scroll bar. Your screen looks like this:

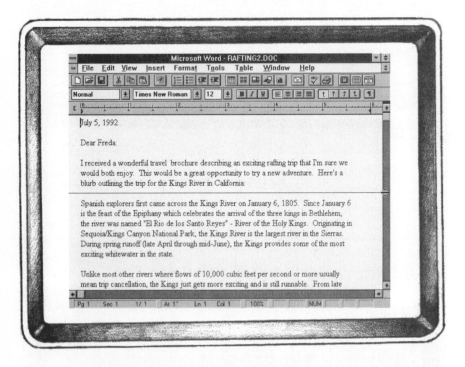

4. When you see the horizontal gray line separating the first and second paragraphs, release the mouse button. The screen looks like this:

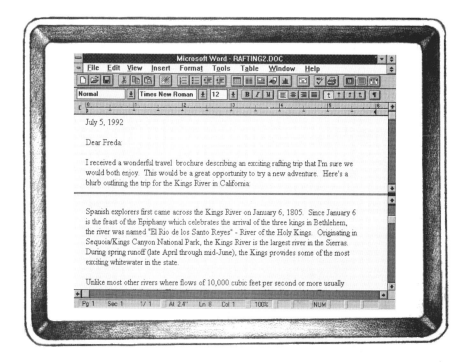

The top half of the screen shows the beginning of the document, followed by a double horizontal line. The text then continues on the bottom half of the screen.

Tip: Another way to split the screen in half is to double-click the split screen bar.

Notice that there are now two vertical scroll bars. Click the down arrow on the *lower* scroll bar. The top half of the screen (the top pane) stays stationary, while the bottom half (the bottom pane) scrolls further down the file.

You can move the cursor from one pane to another by using one of these methods:

- Click in the desired pane
- Press F6

All of the methods for moving the cursor described in Chapter 2 are available while using the split screen.

Copying Text from One Pane to Another

To practice copying text from one part of a file to another location within the same file, perform the following steps:

1. Scroll the text in the bottom pane until the screen looks like this:

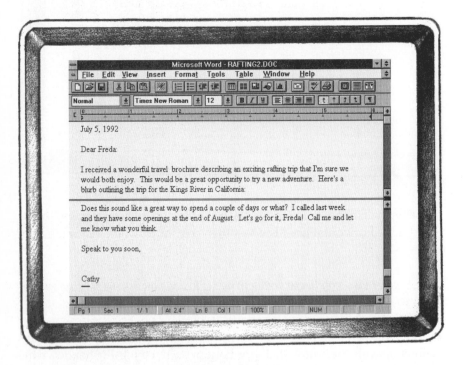

2. Click the top pane and highlight the date.

3. Choose Copy from the Edit menu.

4. Click the bottom pane and position the cursor on the line above "Speak to you soon,".

5. Choose Paste from the Edit menu. The date now appears in both panes.

6. Choose Undo Paste from the Edit menu to remove the date from the bottom window pane.

Splitting a single document into two panes helps you accurately place text, and allows you to compare text in different parts of the document. To return to single-pane view, use one of the following methods:

- Position the mouse on the split screen bar and drag the bar above the up arrow at the top of the vertical scroll bar, then release the mouse

- Double-click the split screen bar

Opening a New Document Window

To open a new document window, follow these steps:

1. With RAFTING2.DOC still active, choose New from the File menu. The New dialog box appears. The template called NORMAL should be highlighted.

Note: The other templates take you, step-by-step, through creating business, academic, and personal types of documents. The use of these other templates is beyond the scope of this book.

2. Click OK. A new document window appears with the name Document2. This is a blank "piece of paper" to use for creating a new file.

The name of the new window is Document2

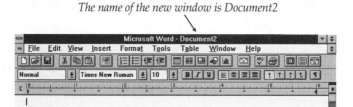

Switching Document Windows

To switch from viewing Document2 to viewing RAFTING2.DOC:

1. Click Window in the menu bar. The Window menu opens.

At the bottom of this short menu is a list of the open documents. Right now, the list consists of Document2 and RAFTING2.DOC. The open documents always appear in alphabetical order. A checkmark appears next to Document2 because it is presently the active document.

2. Click RAFTING2.DOC to make it the active window.

Tip: You can press CTRL-F6 *to switch to the next document, or* CTRL-SHIFT-F6 *to switch to the previous document.*

Viewing More Than One Document at a Time

Both documents presently cover the entire screen, one sitting in front of the other. Copying or cutting text from one document to another is much easier if you can see both files simultaneously. Resizing the windows is one way to accomplish this.

To automatically resize the windows for all open documents, choose Arrange All from the Window menu. The active document occupies the top half of the screen and the second document the lower half.

Note: Because the Arrange All feature arranges windows for all open files, it becomes less useful with more than two active documents. With four files open at once, for example, it's tough to read a file that occupies only a small portion of the screen.

Resizing, Maximizing, and Restoring Windows

As mentioned in Chapter 1, Word for Windows is contained in an application window. The name of the application and any active document, as well as the application's menu bar, appear at the top of the application window.

There are two buttons on the extreme right side of the application's title bar. They are the application minimize button and the application maximize button. Clicking the *application maximize button* enlarges the application window to fill the entire screen. After you enlarge the window, the maximize button is replaced by the restore button, which contains both an up and a down arrow. Click the *restore button* to return the application window to its previous size.

Tip: It might be preferable when learning to use Windows to keep the active application window maximized. Otherwise, if you accidentally clicked some other window, you might make another program active and hide the Word for Windows window.

Clicking the *application minimize button* reduces the application window to an icon. Minimizing applications allows you to quickly move from one open application to another. To turn the application icon back into a window, double-click that icon. Refer to your Windows user's guide for more information about multiple active applications.

If the *document window* is maximized, the application and document share the application's title bar. At the extreme right side of the menu bar is the document restore button. The document restore button works like the application restore button, but it affects the document window. Clicking the *document restore button* returns the document window to its previous size. It also puts the document in its own separate window.

When you choose the Arrange All command, Word for Windows automatically creates separate windows for all open documents. These windows can be manually resized by positioning the mouse pointer on the window borders and dragging. When you choose the Arrange All command, the document restore button is replaced by a *document maximize button.* When you click this button, the document window is returned to full screen.

It's easy to switch between open documents. Right now, the title bar of Document2 is light gray because it is the inactive window. To make Document2 the active window, click anywhere within the Document2 window. The title bar of RAFTING2.DOC is now gray.

To return the active window to full-screen, click the document maximize button, which is the small triangle pointing up, at the extreme right of the title bar.

Copying and Pasting Between Windows

Let's type a letter in the Document2 window to use for practice copying and pasting between windows. Document2 should still be the active document. If you haven't already, return the Document2 window to full-screen (it's easier to type while seeing the entire file onscreen). Then type the following letter:

```
July 16, 1992

Dear Cathy,

I received your letter about the rafting trip. I think it's a fabulous idea to spend
a few days out in nature and get some great exercise steering the rafts. I think I'll
also look forward to the easy parts of the river where I can let my feet dangle over
the side and stare up at a beautiful blue sky.

After our rafting trip, I have an idea for our next adventure. I got a travel newsletter
describing Virginia City, Nevada. It sounded like an interesting old Western place to
investigate. Here's some of the text from the newsletter:

"Colorize one of those 19th century photos of a boom town, substitute tourists' cars
for horse-drawn wagons, and you have modern day Virginia City. The town may look like
a handyman's special, but the whole thing, all that's left from when this was "the
richest place on earth," is a registered historic landmark. In the boom days, in the
1860s and 70s, thousands of miners pulled millions of dollars of silver from beneath
Virginia City."

What do you think? We could investigate the old silver mines as well as the newspaper
office where Mark Twain worked in the 1860s. A few days in the wilderness and a few
more looking at some history sounds like a great vacation to me! The travel between
Virginia City and the Kings River is just a few hours.

Let me know what you think.

See ya,

Freda
```

Save the letter and name it VIRGINIA.DOC. (Refer to Chapter 2 for instructions on how to save a document.) VIRGINIA.DOC and RAFT-ING2.DOC are now the two open documents. Choose Arrange All from the Window menu to resize the windows so you can see both documents at once. Viewing two files simultaneously saves time when parts of one file need to be copied or moved into the other file.

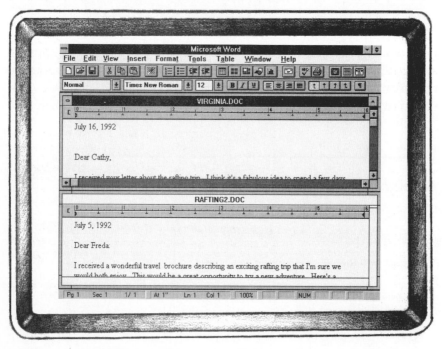

Follow these steps to practice copying text from one document to another:

1. Scroll to make the second paragraph of VIRGINIA.DOC, which begins, "After our rafting trip..." visible on the screen.

2. Select the paragraph. (Refer to Chapter 4 for quick ways to select a paragraph.)

3. Choose Copy from the Edit menu.

4. Click the RAFTING2.DOC window to make it the active window.

5. Move the cursor so it is blinking at the line above "Speak to you soon,".

6. Choose Paste from the Edit menu. The paragraph from VIR-GINIA.DOC should now appear in RAFTING2.DOC.

Save the changes in both files.

What Do They Mean By...?

Active Window   The window that contains the cursor.

Document Maximize Button   This button appears if a window has been resized. It has an up arrow and appears at the extreme right of the title bar of the active window. You use it to maximize the active window to full-screen.

Document Restore Button   If a window is already maximized, this button appears. It has up and down arrows and appears at the extreme right of the menu bar. You use it to return the document window to its previous size.

Inactive Window   A window with a gray or dimmed title bar. It does not contain the cursor.

Open Document   A document that is available onscreen for editing.

Resize a Window   To change the shape of the active window. This action allows you to view the text of one or more open documents at a time.

Split Screen or Split Window   An active document that has been divided into two panes to allow the viewing of two separate sections of the same file.

Using Help in Word for Windows

6

Occasions might come up when you need assistance (besides looking in this book, of course) to find specific commands or learn how to do certain functions. Word for Windows has an excellent help system. Microsoft is so conscious of the need to offer online assistance that it created an entire menu called Help.

The help text is a condensed version of the user's guide, and is meant to be used as a quick reference—a first line of defense.

The Help menu is divided into five menu items:

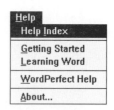

- Help Index
- Getting Started
- Learning Word
- WordPerfect Help
- About

The About option identifies the version of Word for Windows and displays the copyright notice, the license owner and serial number of your copy of the program, the available amount of disk space and memory, and whether a math coprocessor is installed.

This chapter shows you how to use the Help Index and how to navigate through the other help items.

Help Index

There are two ways to access the Help Index:

- Choose Help Index from the Help menu
- Press the F1 key

Either method opens a window named Word Help - WINWORD.HLP.

Note: If you press F1 to view the Help Index, then press F1 again, you will see a screen explaining how to use Help.

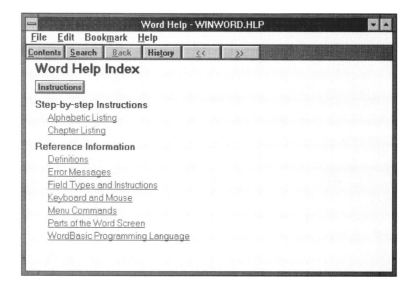

The Word Help window can be resized just like any document window (see Chapter 5 for information about resizing windows).

Note: If your Help window is not large enough for you to see all seven items under Reference Information at once, the window will have a vertical scroll bar so you can scroll to the end of the text.

The Word Help window has a menu bar with four menu items:

- File
- Edit
- Bookmark
- Help

Beneath the menu bar are six buttons:

- Contents
- Search
- Back

- History
- <<
- >>

A dimmed item means that the particular command or button is not available now. The four menu items and the six buttons are discussed later in this chapter.

Topic Headings, Cross-References, and Definitions

The Word for Windows Help system is designed so that you can easily find information about a topic by choosing a topic heading. You can then view information about related topics by choosing a cross-reference, or look at the definition of a term by choosing a definition.

Note: If you do not have a color monitor, disregard any references to green-colored text in the following sections.

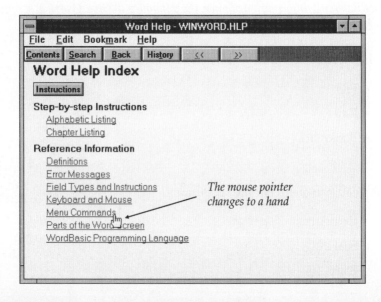

The mouse pointer changes to a hand

Topic Headings

If you point to any of the green-colored topic headings or the button named Instructions, the mouse pointer becomes a hand with a finger pointer. Notice that these headings have a solid underline (whether or not you have a color monitor).

If you click one of these headings, a screen appears with information about the selected topic. The following example explores a topic heading search sequence, in this case, the Save As command.

Tip: *To use the keyboard to access these headings, press* TAB *or* SHIFT-*TAB and then press* ENTER *when the desired topic is selected.*

Click the Reference Information topic heading called Menu Commands. The following screen appears:

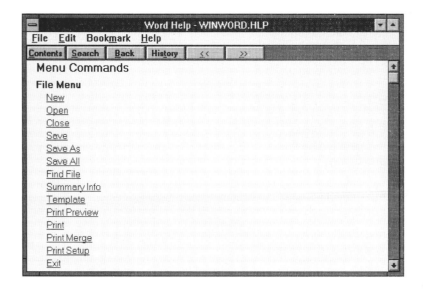

Click the topic heading called Save As. The next screen appears. This window has a vertical scroll bar that allows you to view the rest of the text.

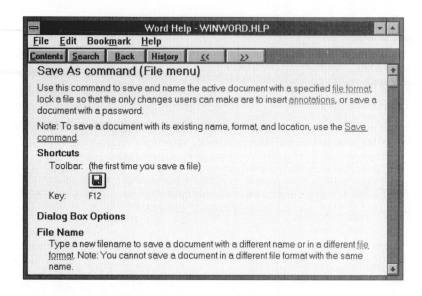

Tip: You can use UP ARROW and DOWN ARROW as well as PAGE UP and PAGE DOWN on the keyboard to view the rest of the window.

Cross-References

Notice the green words within the help text, some with a solid underline and others with a dotted underline. The solid-underlined items are called cross-references. A *cross-reference* is a topic related to the one you are presently viewing.

When you click a cross-reference, Word for Windows Help moves to a new screen with information about the cross-reference. In this example, the Save command is a cross-reference. Cross-references are also listed at the bottom of most topic windows, under the heading "See also."

Definitions

The dotted-underlined items in help text are called *definitions*. If you click a definition, a box appears that displays the definition of that item.

To see a sample definition, click the words "file format" under File Name in the Save As help text.

> **File format**
>
> The format in which data is stored in a file. Word usually stores a document in Word's "Normal" file format, which includes the text and all the formatting applied to the document.
>
> Word can read and save in several file formats, such as WordPerfect, RTF, and earlier versions of Microsoft Word for Windows.

To make the definition disappear, click the mouse again or press ESC.

Help Buttons

The help buttons are located directly below the Help menu bar. To access any of these items, click the desired button.

Contents Button

The Contents button returns you to the Help Index.

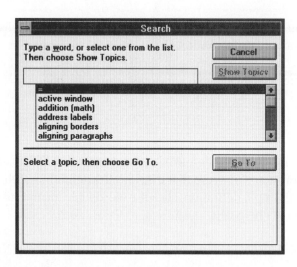

Search Button

§earch

The Search button allows you to inquire about other available topics. Clicking the Search button brings up the Search dialog box.

To choose a topic to search for, perform the following steps. In this example, you search for the Cut command.

1. Scroll through the alphabetical list of topics in the Search dialog box and click the desired topic. Alternatively, type the name of the topic you want and Word for Windows jumps to highlight the command you type.

    In this case, click the cutting text topic, or type **cut** and Word for Windows highlights the cutting text topic.

Note: If you type a topic that Word for Windows doesn't recognize, it leaves you at the closest topic alphabetically to the topic requested.

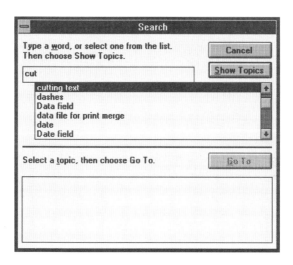

2. Click the Show Topics button.

3. At the bottom of the dialog box, a list of related topics appears that contains information pertaining to your topic. Click the topic you want to read about, then click Go To and Word for Windows displays that screen.

Tip: *You can also double-click the topic to see the related topics.*

In this case, click Moving text, then click the Go To button.

Tip: *You can double-click one of the related topics to jump straight to that screen.*

Back Button

Word for Windows keeps track of each screen you've viewed while browsing through the help screens. Click the Back button to move to the previous screen.

History Button

If you click the History button, Word for Windows displays a chronological list of all the screens you've viewed, with the most recent at the top of the list. To return to a topic, double-click the topic.

<< and >> Buttons

The << and >> buttons display the previous or next topic in a series of related topics. Using the Save As example, click << (previous) to display the Save help screen. If you are looking at the Save As screen, clicking >> (next) shows the File Sharing help screen. The << and >> buttons are another way to browse through associated subject matter.

Help Menu Bar

As mentioned previously, the Word Help window has a menu bar with four menu items. These menu items are File, Edit, Bookmark, and Help.

File

The File menu contains the following options:

- The Open command opens a help file. The default help file is called WINWORD.HLP, but you can open other help files from Windows itself, if you desire.

- The Print Topic command allows you to print the help screen for a topic.

- The Print Setup command allows you to choose which printer you wish to use for printing the help screen.

- The Exit command exits help and returns to the document.

Edit

The Edit menu includes a Copy command that allows you to copy text from the help screen. When you exit help and return to the document, you can use the Paste command to put the help text into your file.

The Edit menu's other command is called Annotate. This command allows you to add your own comments to the help topics.

Bookmark

Just like a bookmark in a book, the Bookmark command marks specific references in Help. Once a specific help topic is bookmarked, you can return to it quickly by choosing it from the Bookmark menu.

To create a bookmark for Save As:

1. Go to the Save As help screen.

2. Choose Define from the Bookmark menu.

3. Click OK.

Now when you choose the Bookmark menu, you can quickly go to the help screen for Save As because Save As is now a menu item under Bookmark.

To delete a Bookmark:

1. Choose Define from the Bookmark menu.
2. Click the item to be deleted.
3. Click the Delete button.
4. Click OK.

Help

The Help menu on the menu bar has an option called How to Use Help. This option gives many cross-references on how to maneuver around help.

If you choose How to Use Help, a new button appears called Glossary. It replaces the << and >> buttons. If you choose Glossary, an alphabetically arranged window of definitions appears.

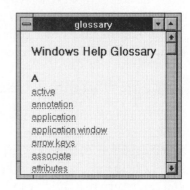

Click any of the definitions to see an explanation for that item. To close the Glossary window, click in an area outside the Glossary window.

The quickest way to exit from How to Use Help is

1. Click the History button.
2. Scroll until you see *WINWORD:Microsoft Word Help*.
3. Double-click it to go back to the Help Index.

Context-Sensitive Help

Context-sensitive help is a Word for Windows feature that allows you to get help about a dialog box without having to navigate through the Help

Index. To use context-sensitive help, press F1 when a dialog box is displayed. Help information about that dialog box appears. From this point, you can navigate the help screens as mentioned previously.

Help on a Command

You can also get help on a menu item without having to access the Help menu. If you want to get help on a particular menu item:

1. Press SHIFT-F1. Your pointer changes to an arrow with a question mark.

2. Click the desired menu option. You go directly to that help topic.

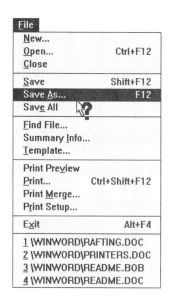

Note: SHIFT-F1 *cannot be used to access the help screen for dimmed items on the menu. To access help on dimmed items, point to the desired item and hold down the mouse button. Then, while holding down the button, press* F1.

Getting Started

Getting Started is a very good tutorial for the basic skills needed to use Word for Windows. If you choose Getting Started while you're in the middle of a document, the tutorial will not affect your work. It suspends your current work and brings you back when you exit.

To activate the tutorial, choose Getting Started from the Help menu. The following screen appears:

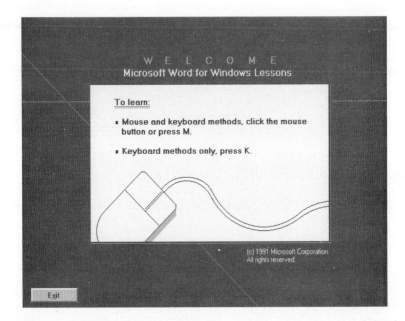

To learn to use the mouse commands, click the mouse or press M. Press K to learn to use the Word for Windows keyboard equivalents. Either option sends you to this screen:

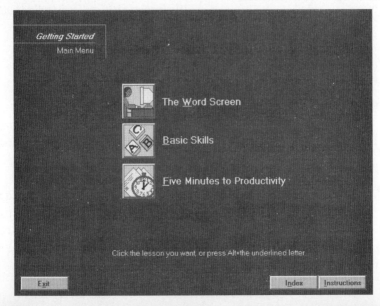

Click the item you want to learn about. You can display an index of topics covered by Getting Started by clicking the Index button at the bottom-right corner of the screen.

Once you're within a lesson, click the right arrow at the bottom-right corner of the screen to move to the next screen. To go back a screen, click the left arrow. Your keyboard LEFT ARROW and RIGHT ARROW keys work as well.

To exit from Getting Started while in a lesson, click the Controls button at the bottom-right corner of the screen. The Controls dialog box appears. Click the Exit button.

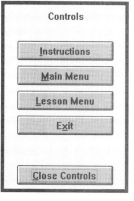

Learning Word

The other help tutorial is called Learning Word. It contains lessons that go beyond the scope of Getting Started. Learning Word explains a wider variety of features and details than a quick how-to. To activate the tutorial, choose Learning Word from the Help menu. The following screen appears:

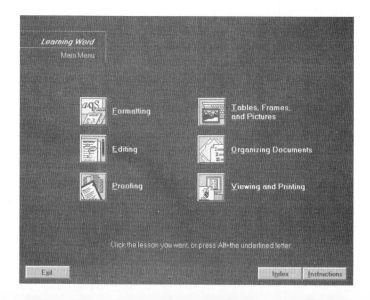

Navigating features, such as the Index button, the Controls button, and directional buttons, are also available in this tutorial. And, just like Getting Started, Learning Word returns you to your document when you exit. To exit from Learning Word while in a lesson, click the Controls button, then click the Exit button in the Controls dialog box.

WordPerfect Help

WordPerfect Help is available for people who have previously used Word-Perfect 5.0 or 5.1. This help function explains how Word for Windows performs similar WordPerfect commands. The Help for WordPerfect Users dialog box appears when you select WordPerfect Help.

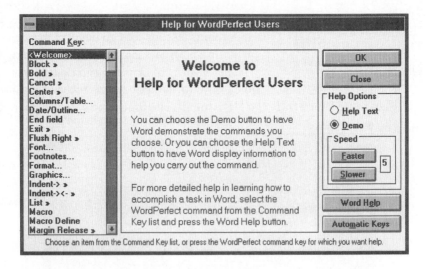

There are a number of ways to use the Help for WordPerfect Users dialog box. They are listed as follows

- Click a command from the Command Key list to see information about how you use that command in Word for Windows.

- Some Command Key topics are followed by an ellipsis (...). Double-click one of these topics to show the WordPerfect commands associated with that topic. You can then click one of these WordPerfect commands to find out how to perform it in Word for Windows.

- Type a WordPerfect keyboard command to see how to perform that command in Word for Windows. For example, if you press SHIFT-F7 (WordPerfect's Print command), you see how to print in Word for Windows.

There are several help options in the Help for WordPerfect Users window. If the Demo Button under Help Options is selected, Word for Windows performs any Command Key command you double-click. Use the Speed option to set how fast Word for Windows moves from one step to another when performing the command. The Demo option can be tricky, because Word for Windows not only shows where the command is but also performs the command. Unless you want the program to demonstrate the commands for you, keep Help Options set to Help Text.

In the bottom-right corner of the dialog box is the Automatic Keys button. With Automatic Keys active, when you exit from WordPerfect Help and press a WordPerfect function key command, a WordPerfect Help screen appears and tells you how Word for Windows performs that function. To disable Automatic Keys, choose WordPerfect Help again from the Help menu and click Disable Automatic.

Just above the Automatic Keys button is the Word Help button. Clicking the Word Help button opens the Word Help Index discussed earlier in this chapter. You can navigate around Word help as needed. When you are ready to return to WordPerfect Help, choose Exit from the File menu.

What Do They Mean By...?

Help Index   The main starting point for investigating help topics in Word for Windows. It is found in the Help menu.

Cross-Reference   A solid-underlined heading that is related to the topic presently being viewed. Click a cross-reference to view help information about that related topic.

Definition   A dotted-underlined item that, when clicked, displays a box with a definition of that item.

Character
Formatting

In the letters you have created so far, you have typed the text, saved it, made corrections, and moved text from one document to another. Once you are satisfied with the content of the file, you might start thinking about how the text looks, or about changing the display of words to draw the reader's eye to a specific place in your document. This feature is known as *character formatting*. Another handy feature is the ability to change the *case* of text, to go from uppercase to lowercase or to first letter capitalization.

To change the appearance of existing text, highlight the text and then choose Character from the Format menu. If the text is not selected first, any changes made in the Character dialog box affect only new text that is typed from the present cursor position. (See Chapter 3 for text selection commands.)

Before adding character enhancements, you should verify that your printer can print all of them. Experiment with some sample text and then print your samples. If what you see on the screen does not match what comes out on paper, check your printer manual or contact the printer manufacturer. These sources can tell you what your printer can and cannot produce.

Character Formats

Character formatting involves changes in the following categories:

- Font
- Point size

- Style
- Color
- Spacing
- Superscript and subscript

The next sections look at these categories more closely.

Font

Microsoft Windows has several different design sets of alphabet characters available. Each design set is called a font. A *font* is a set of uppercase and lowercase letters, numerals, punctuation marks, and/or other unique symbols that has a unified design. Word for Windows uses all the fonts provided by Windows.

Arial	Σψμβολ (Symbol)
Times New Roman	✦✠ℵ◻◻◻✠◻ℵ◦ (Wingdings)
Courier	*Script*

Some fonts are monospaced; others are proportional spaced. *Monospaced* means that each letter occupies the same amount of space on a line; therefore, the letter "i" takes up as much space as the letter "w." A commonly used monospaced font is Courier. *Proportional spaced* means that characters take up different amounts of space on a line. In this case, the wider letter "w" occupies more space on a line than the letter "i." One of the proportional spaced fonts that comes with Windows 3.1 is Arial. The two type styles look quite different.

`This is a monospaced font, Courier.`

This is a proportional spaced font, Arial.

If your printer has the capability to use proportional spaced fonts, your text can look almost like it's typeset, or professionally published, when printed. The monospaced fonts often resemble the output of a typewriter.

Fonts are a good way to set the tone or mood of the documents you create. A party invitation may look more attractive with a script-type font, for example, while a business proposal looks more professional with a proportional or monospaced font. There is no right or wrong font, only the ones you like. Experiment and see which look best to you.

Note: Some of the illustrations in this chapter show the font names for an Apple LaserWriter IIf printer. If you do not have this printer, some of the font names listed on your screen may be different.

Let's try some character formatting and different fonts on the letter RAFTING2.DOC.

1. Open RAFTING2.DOC.

2. Select the first paragraph, which begins "I received a wonderful...."

3. Choose Character from the Format menu. The Character dialog box appears.

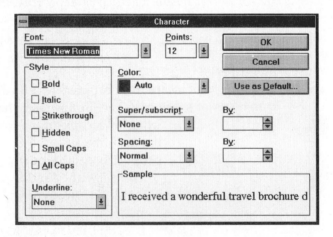

To view the available fonts, click the down arrow next to the Font box. A drop-down list box opens with the font names in alphabetical order.

4. Scroll to the top of the list and click Arial. Notice the change in the Sample box in the bottom-right corner of the Character dialog box. The Sample box shows how the text will look if you click OK to select the font.

5. Click OK to select Arial and return to the editing screen. Click an empty part of the screen to deselect the paragraph so you can see the font change. Your screen should look like this:

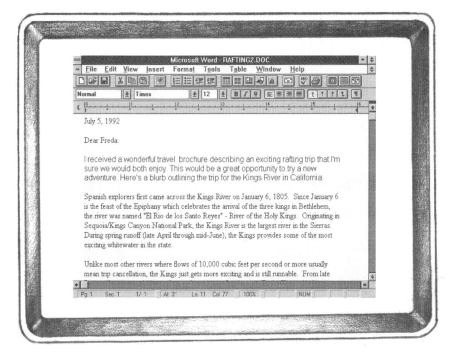

If you want to use a keyboard equivalent to change fonts, follow these steps:

1. Select the text.

2. Press CTRL-F.

3. Type the font name.

4. Press ENTER.

Printer, TrueType, and Screen Fonts

In the Font drop-down list box, you may have noticed that some fonts have a printer or double-T icon (**T**) to the left of their names. (If you are using Windows 3.0, you won't have double-T fonts.) The fonts with the printer icon are printer fonts, the fonts with the double-T icon are TrueType fonts, and the fonts without an icon are screen fonts.

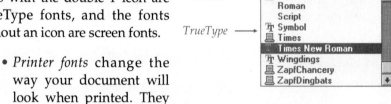

- *Printer fonts* change the way your document will look when printed. They are built into your printer or can be temporarily stored in the printer's RAM.

- *Screen fonts* are the fonts you see on the screen.

- *TrueType fonts* are the same when printed as they are onscreen.

You may or may not have a matching screen font for a given printer font. If there is no screen font to match the printer font you have chosen, Windows chooses a similar screen font or TrueType font to display your text onscreen. Depending on the font substitution, what you see on the screen may not look exactly like the printed document. If you select a TrueType font, on the other hand, the document looks the same onscreen as on paper. TrueType fonts come with Windows 3.1. It's a good idea to create and print your documents using either printer fonts or TrueType fonts. Screen fonts look fine on your screen, but your printer might not know how to print them properly. If you try to

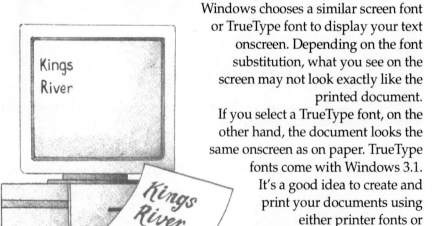

Printer fonts ⟶

TrueType Fonts

print using a screen font, the printer has to create *each letter* of the file one dot at a time. This is a time-consuming process. In addition, screen fonts come in predetermined character sizes, and the way they look on the screen may or may not be the same as they appear on paper.

Point Size

The size of characters can be made smaller or larger to emphasize certain text. The different sizes are measured in typographic units called *points*. One point is equal to 1/72-inch. Point sizes in Word for Windows range from tiny 4-point to giant 127-point, in half-point increments.

Some printer fonts are measured in characters per inch, or cpi, rather than in points; cpi is a horizontal measurement of how many characters fit in an inch. With cpi printer fonts, the *larger* the number, the *smaller* the character is. cpi fonts come in set sizes—for example, Courier 10cpi—and the

size can't be adjusted.

If you try to change the point size for a cpi font, it won't have any effect on the printed characters or how the characters appear onscreen.

If your printer uses only fonts with character-per-inch measurements, experiment with these fonts to see what they look like when printed. Remember, if you are using Windows 3.1, TrueType fonts are an alternative to your built-in printer fonts.

10 Point
12 point
14 point
18 point
24 point
36 point
48 point
72 point

For practice:

1. Highlight the first paragraph of RAFTING2.DOC again.

2. Choose Character from the Format menu.

3. Click the down arrow next to the Points box to open the drop-down list box. Scroll down the list to see the entire point-size range.

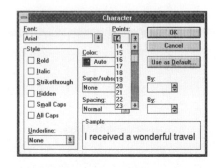

4. Choose 14 and click OK. Notice how the size of each word in the paragraph increases.

Tip: If you want to use a size that is not listed, such as 15.5, drag the pointer over the number in the Points box, press BACKSPACE *to delete the existing size, type in the desired size, and click OK.*

The keyboard equivalents for changing point size are

- To change point size, press CTRL-P, type the new number, and press ENTER.

- To increase point size by one point, press CTRL-F2.

- To decrease point size by one point, press CTRL-SHIFT-F2.

Style

The Style item in the Character dialog box has seven options you can select to change the style of your text. They are

- Bold
- Italic
- Strikethrough

bold   *italic*

~~strikethrough~~   hidden

ALL CAPS   SMALL CAPS

underline   word underline

double underline

- Hidden
- Small Caps
- All Caps
- Underline

For practice, highlight each of the following words in the first paragraph of RAFTING2.DOC and change their character style by clicking the appropriate checkbox and clicking OK:

Bold	rafting
Italic	opportunity
Strikethrough	in California
Hidden	great
Small Caps	Kings River
All Caps	wonderful

Look at the document and note each change after you click OK.

Underline doesn't have a checkbox like the other options. To underline text, you select the text as usual, then you choose an underline style from the Underline drop-down list box.

The underline options are

- None
- Single
- Words Only (the spaces between words are not underlined)
- Double

For practice, put a Words Only underline on the second sentence of the first paragraph of RAFTING2.DOC.

The keyboard equivalents for character styles are

Bold	CTRL-B
Italic	CTRL-I
Hidden Text	CTRL-H

Small Caps	CTRL-K
All Caps	CTRL-A
Underline	CTRL-U
Word Underline	CTRL-W
Double Underline	CTRL-D

There is no keyboard equivalent for strikethrough.

Color

You use the Color item to change the color of text onscreen. First highlight the text and then choose a color from the Color drop-down list box. If you do not have a color monitor, you might see shades of gray if you change text color.

If you have a color printer, the Color item also changes the color that the text prints. Many color printers have a printable test page so you can see the range of available colors. Use this test page to match the printer colors to those available in Word for Windows. If you do not have a color printer, then changing the text color will not have the desired effect on paper.

Spacing

The Spacing item allows you to change the space between characters in highlighted text, moving them closer together or farther apart.

Normal
E x p a n d e d   (by 6 points)
Condensed   (by 1.5 points)

You'll probably use the Spacing option primarily for headlines. You can adjust the spacing by using one of these methods:

- Choose Expanded or Condensed from the Spacing drop-down list box. The default measurement for Expanded is 3 points, and Condensed starts at 1.75 points. You can click the change buttons next to the By box to adjust these amounts. Spacing can be expanded by up to 14 points and condensed by up to 1.75 points.

- Click the change buttons adjacent to the By box. Clicking the up change button automatically changes the spacing to Expanded. Clicking the down change button automatically changes the spacing to Condensed.

To return to Normal, you have two options:

- Choose Normal from the Spacing drop-down list box.
- Click the change buttons to return the spacing to zero points.

To practice what you've learned so far:

1. Highlight the date at the beginning of the letter in RAFTING2.DOC.
2. Change the font to Arial, 16 point, bold.
3. Change the spacing to Expanded by 5 points.

Baseline

Super/subscript

$$E=mc^2 \leftarrow$$

$$H_2O$$

Superscripts and subscripts are often used in scientific documentation. An example of a superscript is $E=mc^2$; a subscript character appears in H_2O. In each case, the number 2 is either above or below the baseline. The *baseline* is the imaginary line that the text is sitting on.

To create superscript or subscript text, you follow these steps:

1. Select the text to be formatted.
2. Choose Character from the Format menu.

3. Click the down arrow beside the Super/subscript box to open the drop-down list box, and then choose either Superscript or Subscript.

4. If you want to increase the distance the text is placed above or below the baseline, click the change buttons in the By box adjacent to the Super/subscript box. Notice the changes in the Sample box.

5. Click OK.

To practice applying superscript and subscript formatting:

1. Go to the end of RAFTING2.DOC and press ENTER twice.

2. Type E=MC2 and press ENTER.

3. Type H2SO4 and press ENTER.

4. Highlight the "2" after the "C" in "E=MC2".

5. Choose Character from the Format menu.

6. Click the down arrow next to the Super/sub-script box to open the drop-down list box.

7. Click Superscript and click OK.

8. Select the "2" after the "H" in "H2SO4".

9. Choose Character from the Format menu.

10. Click the down arrow next to the Super/subscript box to open the drop-down list box.

11. Click Subscript and change the amount to 4 points.

12. Click OK.

13. Make the "4" in the same line subscript by 6 points.

Here are the keyboard equivalents for superscript and subscript:

Superscript by 3 points	CTRL-SHIFT-=
Subscript by 3 points	CTRL-=

Changing the Case of Characters

You can change the case of highlighted characters by using a keyboard equivalent. It is possible, for example, to change a lowercase word to uppercase or to capitalize the first letter of each word in a selection. This feature saves you from having to go back and retype each word.

To change case, select the text, then press SHIFT-F3. Pressing SHIFT-F3 cycles you through three options—lowercase, uppercase, and first character uppercase. Each time you press SHIFT-F3, the text changes to the next option. For example, if your selected text is all lowercase and you press SHIFT-F3, it changes to all uppercase. If you press SHIFT-F3 again, it changes to first character uppercase. Cycle through the options until you get the one you want.

For practice, highlight the first sentence of the second paragraph in RAFTING2.DOC and press SHIFT-F3 to see the changes. When you're done, close RAFTING2.DOC and *do not* save the changes.

What Do They Mean By...?

Character Formatting   The appearance of text in a document.

Font   A set of uppercase and lowercase letters having a unified design and including numerals, punctuation marks, and/or some unique symbols.

Printer Fonts   Fonts that are included with your printer or can be temporarily available to the printer when requested.

Screen Fonts   Fonts that represent a character set on the computer screen.

TrueType Fonts   Fonts that appear the same onscreen as when they are printed. TrueType fonts are included with Windows 3.1.

Paragraph Formatting

In Chapter 7, you formatted selected words in a document to make them stand out. This chapter looks at formatting paragraphs. Altering the appearance of paragraphs can change the look of the entire document. For example, double spacing a paragraph can make it more readable, and center aligning a memo title can draw the reader's eye.

Paragraph formatting includes the following:

- Indentation
- Alignment
- Line Spacing
- Tabs

What Is a Paragraph?

Word for Windows considers a *paragraph* to be a line or several lines of text that ends when you press ENTER. For example, let's say you type a person's name on one line, their street address on a second line, and their city, state, and ZIP code on a third line, pressing ENTER after each line. Word for Windows sees this mailing label as three paragraphs. If you don't press ENTER, Word for Windows decides how many words fit on a line, and wraps the remaining words to the next line.

Paragraph Symbol

Word for Windows puts a special character at the end of a paragraph so it knows where the paragraph finishes. This character looks like an editor's paragraph symbol: ¶. You can set up Word for Windows so that you can see the paragraph symbol onscreen. This can be helpful if you need to highlight a paragraph for formatting because it's easy to see where the paragraph ends and ensure that you have all the text selected. In addition, you can see if you have extra paragraph symbols in your document, and select and delete them as you would any other character.

Note: Even though you can see the paragraph symbols onscreen, they won't print on the printer.

On the far-right side of the ribbon is a button with a paragraph symbol on it. This is the Hide/Show button. It allows you to show or hide all the special characters, including the ¶ symbol. Click that button once to show all the symbols.

Retrieve RAFTING2.DOC for the upcoming practice exercises. After opening the file, your screen should look like this:

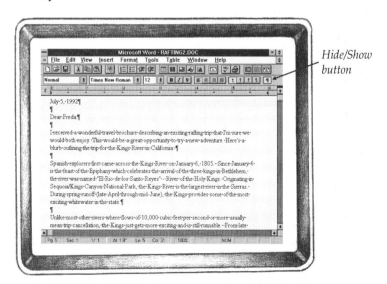

Hide/Show
button

You can see the paragraph symbols in the document. You can also see a small dot between each word. The dots represent each time the SPACEBAR is pressed. All of the items on the ribbon other than the Hide/Show button will be covered in Chapter 10.

Paragraph Basics

You can set paragraph formatting the way you want and Word for Windows uses that format for all the paragraphs you type until you change it to something else. If you format a paragraph for double-spacing, for example, and you press ENTER at the end of the paragraph, then the formatting for that paragraph (double-spaced) continues to the next paragraph you type. To change the format of an existing paragraph, highlight it and change only its format.

Note: If you are changing the format of a single paragraph, you don't actually have to highlight the text. Instead, put your cursor anywhere within the paragraph and then issue the format commands. When formatting more than one paragraph at time, you do need to highlight the desired text.

Copying Paragraph Formats

The formatting information for a paragraph is kept in its ¶ symbol. You can copy the format of one paragraph and paste it onto another paragraph by copying and pasting the ¶ symbol. Copying the ¶ symbol can be a great time saver. It works basically the same way you copy and paste text.

To copy paragraph formats:

1. Highlight the paragraph symbol at the end of the desired paragraph. This assumes you have already made the symbols visible onscreen.

2. Choose Copy from the Edit menu.

3. Highlight the paragraph symbol at the end of the target paragraph.

4. Choose Paste from the Edit menu.

Indentation

The indentation feature in Word for Windows allows you to adjust the location of a paragraph's first line in relation to the left margin, or to adjust the location of the entire paragraph in relation to the left and right margins. The indentation level can be set at the beginning of the paragraph, and Word for Windows automatically indents each line as you type. You might want to use indentation for direct quotations, dates, letter closings, numbered lists, or bulleted lists.

- Travel
- Adventure
- White water

JULY 5, 1992

Sincerely yours,

Now is the time...

You can change paragraph indents by using the Paragraph dialog box, the ruler, or keyboard equivalents. To experiment with indentation, highlight the paragraph of RAFTING2.DOC that begins, "Spanish explorers first came...," and follow the instructions in the following sections.

Indentation Using the Paragraph Dialog Box

The Paragraph dialog box has several setting areas. This part of the chapter discusses those that relate to indentation. The settings for spacing and alignment are discussed later in this chapter. To read about pagination and line numbers, take a look at your Word for Windows User's Guide.

Practice changing indentation with the Paragraph dialog box by following these steps:

1. Choose Paragraph from the Format menu. The Paragraph dialog box appears.

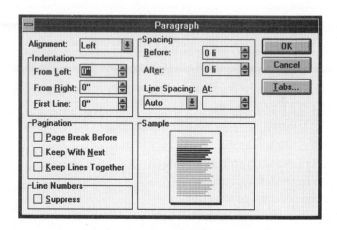

The settings for indentation are in the upper-left corner of the dialog box, under the word "Indentation." The From Left option allows you to set the entire paragraph's distance from the left margin. From Right lets you set the paragraph's distance from the right margin. First Line lets you specify how far the first line of the paragraph will be indented from the left margin.

2. Click the change button at the right side of the First Line box to increase the First Line measurement to .7".

3. Change the From Right measurement to 1".

Notice how the darkened paragraph changes in the Sample box. This paragraph reflects the changes you are making.

4. Click OK to return to the document.

Your paragraph should look like the following:

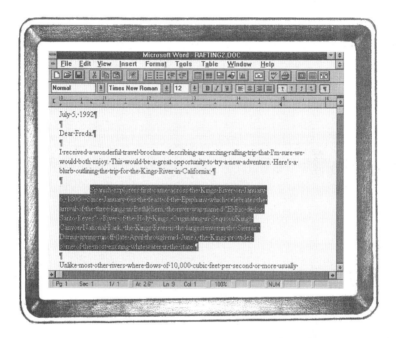

The first line of the paragraph is now indented .7 inches, and the entire right side is moved in by one inch.

Choose Undo Formatting from the Edit menu to return the paragraph to its original indent.

Indentation Using the Ruler

Using the mouse and the ruler to adjust paragraph indents bypasses the Paragraph dialog box. If you feel comfortable with the mouse, this method allows you to change indents quickly.

Notice the two small triangles on the ruler beneath the 0" mark, as well as the larger single triangle by the 6" mark.

First-line indent marker

Left indent marker

Right indent marker

Underneath the 0" mark, the top triangle represents the first-line indent. The bottom triangle represents the rest of the paragraph's left indent. The triangle at the 6" mark represents the paragraph's right indent.

You change indents by dragging these triangles on the ruler. Here are some rules you should keep in mind while dragging:

- The top-left triangle (the first-line indent marker) drags independently of the bottom-left triangle.

- The bottom-left triangle (the left indent marker) drags the top triangle with it, *unless* you press SHIFT while dragging.

- The right triangle (the right indent marker) drags independently of both left triangles.

For practice indenting with the ruler, follow these steps:

1. Position the cursor within the second paragraph of RAFT-ING2.DOC.

2. Point at the right indent marker.

3. Drag it to the left so the triangle is at the 5" mark on the ruler, then release the mouse.

4. Drag the first-line indent marker to .75" and release the mouse.

Your screen should look much the same as it did when you made these changes from the Paragraph dialog box. Choose Undo Formatting from the Edit menu to return the paragraph to its original indent.

Hanging Indents

A paragraph with a *hanging indent* is a paragraph whose first line begins to the left of the rest of the paragraph. This is sometimes called an outdent. Hanging indents are commonly used for numbered lists and bulleted lists.

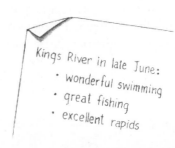

Kings River in late June:
- wonderful swimming
- great fishing
- excellent rapids

To make a hanging indent, hold down the SHIFT key and drag the left indent marker to the desired place on the ruler.

For practice:

1. Position the cursor in the first sentence of the third paragraph of RAFTING2.DOC. It begins with, "Unlike most other rivers..."

2. Point at the left indent marker (the bottom-left triangle on the ruler).

3. Hold down SHIFT, then drag the mouse until the left indent marker is at .5".

4. Release the mouse and view the changes in the paragraph.

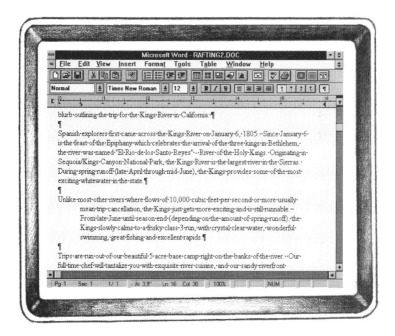

5. Press CTRL-G to decrease the indent, returning it to its original place. (You will learn more keyboard equivalents in the next section.)

Indentation Using Keyboard Equivalents

There are several keyboard equivalents for indenting paragraphs:

Format	Keyboard Equivalent
Normal	CTRL-Q
.5" Hanging Indent	CTRL-T
.5" Decrease Hanging Indent	CTRL-G
.5" Increase Left Indent	CTRL-N
.5" Decrease Left Indent	CTRL-M

A Normal paragraph is the format for a paragraph *before* you manually change the format. By pressing CTRL-Q, you remove any alignment and spacing changes, as well as any newly-created tab stops.

The cursor can be anywhere in the paragraph (the entire paragraph does not need to be selected) to use the keyboard equivalents.

Alignment

Paragraph alignment refers to how a paragraph lines up horizontally. There are four types of alignment in Word for Windows:

- *Left*   Each line of text aligns straight down the left margin, and the right side of the paragraph is ragged. (*Ragged* means that if a word falls short of the margin, it stays there; extra spaces aren't added between the words in the line to make that word meet the margin.)

- *Centered*   Each line of the paragraph is centered between the left and right margins.

- *Right*   Each line of text aligns straight down the right margin, and the left side of the paragraph is ragged.

- *Justified*   Each line of text aligns straight down both the left and right margins (except the last line of the paragraph, which is left aligned). Space is added between words to fill out short lines. Because there is an unequal number of letters on each line, the spacing between words varies from line to line.

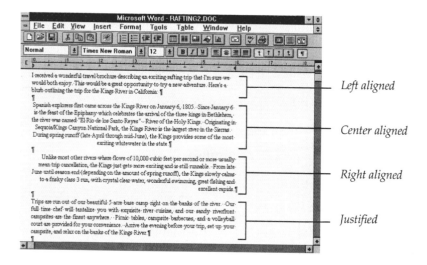

Left aligned

Center aligned

Right aligned

Justified

Note: *Center-aligned text is often used for headlines or notices, right-aligned is sometimes used for dates or correspondence addresses, and justified text is used in newspapers to provide a crisp format.*

As you work through the following examples, you will format paragraphs with each of the four alignments. You can choose paragraph alignments by using

- The Paragraph dialog box
- Keyboard equivalents
- The ribbon

Alignment Using the Paragraph Dialog Box

In the Paragraph dialog box, the paragraph alignment settings are located in the upper-left corner. To see the different options, click the down arrow next to the Alignment box. The drop-down list box opens.

Alignment:

Left	↓

Left
Centered
Right
Justified

Click the desired alignment, then click OK. Remember, if you are changing the format of a single paragraph, position the cursor *anywhere* within the paragraph. You do not need to select the entire paragraph.

For practice:

- Make the second paragraph of RAFTING2.DOC center aligned.
- Make the third paragraph right aligned.
- Make the fourth paragraph justified.

Alignment Using Keyboard Equivalents

The following table lists the keyboard equivalents for changing alignment:

Format	Keyboard Equivalent
Left	CTRL-L
Center	CTRL-E
Right	CTRL-R
Justified	CTRL-J

For practice:

1. Position the cursor in the second paragraph of RAFTING2.DOC. This paragraph should be center aligned.
2. Press CTRL-Q to reset the paragraph to left aligned.
3. Position the cursor in the third paragraph (right aligned) and press CTRL-Q.
4. Position the cursor in the fourth paragraph (justified) and press CTRL-Q.
5. Return to each of these paragraphs and use the keyboard equivalents to make the second, third, and fourth paragraphs centered, right aligned, and justified, respectively.

Alignment Using the Ribbon

Paragraph alignment using the ribbon is covered in Chapter 10.

Line Spacing

Word for Windows allows you to adjust the line spacing above, below, and within a paragraph. The default settings are single-space with no additional spacing above or below the paragraph, as well as Auto line spacing within the paragraph. *Auto line spacing* adjusts to fit the tallest character on a line. If a paragraph consists primarily of 12-point type, but one line contains a word in 24-point type, that one line adjusts its spacing to accommodate the 24-point word. Virtually all commands for line spacing are found in the Paragraph dialog box.

There are several reasons that you might want to change line spacing in a document. For example, you could indent a short quote or instructional steps and add space above and below them to make them stand out. Also, double-line spacing is often used in manuscripts because the extra space between lines makes it easier to mark items that need to be changed.

Before and After Paragraph Spacing

Choose Paragraph from the Format menu and notice the Before and After options in the Spacing section of the Paragraph dialog box. The Before and After options allow you to set the amount of space above and below a paragraph. The space is measured in lines, abbreviated li. To change the line spacing above or below a paragraph, either type the amount of lines you want into the Before or After box, or click the change buttons at the right of the boxes to increase or decrease the line measurement.

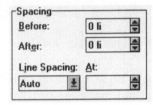

For practice:

1. Increase the Before measurement until it reaches 2 li.

2. Increase the After measurement until it reaches 1 li.

3. Click OK to see the changes.

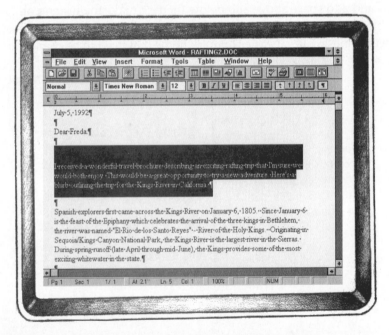

Press CTRL-Q to return the paragraph to normal spacing.

Line Spacing Within the Paragraph

With the Paragraph dialog box open, click the down arrow to the right of
the Line Spacing box to open the drop-down list box. The line spacing
options are Auto, Single, 1.5 Lines, Double, At Least, and Exactly.

Auto line spacing means there is no fixed amount of space. The space
between lines varies depending on the tallest character in that line. Therefore, a 24-point word in the middle of a line of 12-point text causes Word
for Windows to adjust the line spacing so that there is enough space for the
24-point word.

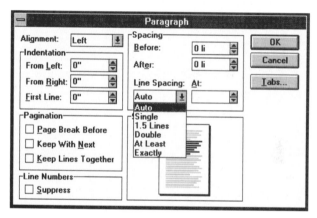

The Exactly line spacing option tells Word for Windows not to adjust for
larger type within a line. Notice the contrast between Auto and Exactly in
the two illustrations.

¶
Spanish·explorers·first·came·across·the·Kings·River·on·January·6,·1805.··Since·January·6·
is·the·feast·of·the·Epiphany·which·celebrates·the·arrival·of·the·three·kings·in·Bethlehem,·
the·river·was·named·"El·Rio·de·los·Santo·Reyes"··River·of·the·Holy·Kings.··Originating·in·

Sequoia/Kings·Canyon·National·Park,·the·Kings·   ⟵ *Auto*

River·is·the·largest·river·in·the·Sierras.·During·spring·runoff·(late·April·through·mid-June),·
the·Kings·provides·some·of·the·most·exciting·whitewater·in·the·state.¶   *Exactly*
¶

¶
Spanish·explorers·first·came·across·the·Kings·River·on·January·6,·1805.··Since·January·6·
is·the·feast·of·the·Epiphany·which·celebrates·the·arrival·of·the·three·kings·in·Bethlehem,·
the·river·was·named·"El·Rio·de·los·Santo·Reyes"··River·of·the·Holy·Kings.··Originating·in·
Sequoia/Kings·Canyon·National·Park,·the·Kings·
River·is·the·largest·river·in·the·Sierras.·During·spring·runoff·(late·April·through·mid-June),·
the·Kings·provides·some·of·the·most·exciting·whitewater·in·the·state.¶
¶

Note: *Your document will have the same line spacing when printed as it does onscreen.*

You can specify a line spacing amount by using the At box. If you want triple spacing, for example, click the change button in the At box until the number in it reaches 3 li. Notice the Line Spacing box now says At Least. You could have chosen At Least from the Line Spacing drop-down list first, and then clicked the change buttons in the At box. Either method changes the line spacing within the paragraph. Observe the changes in the Sample box as well.

Click OK to see the triple-spaced text.

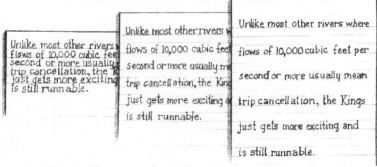

Tip: *You'll probably want to leave the line spacing at Auto unless you need double-, triple- or 1.5-line spacing.*

Press CTRL-Q to return the paragraph to normal spacing.

Tabs

Tabs are used to set up aligned columns of text. If you need to create one column with names and a second column with numbers, for example, setting tabs is a way to line up the items properly.

Tip: *Tabs are useful for small amounts of text and a small number of columns. If your task requires many columns and complicated formatting, the Table feature is best suited for the job. The Table feature is beyond the scope of this book, but you can find more information about it in your Word for Windows user's guide.*

When you press TAB, the cursor jumps to the next tab stop, and a tab character fills the space. The character looks like an arrow pointing to the right. If the Hide/Show button discussed earlier is in Show mode, as it is for the illustrations in this chapter, you will see the tab symbol onscreen.

Caution: If you use the SPACEBAR *to align text, you might be in for a surprise when you print your document. Depending on the font used, the text will look like it's lined up correctly onscreen, but when printed, your columns will not be aligned. If you use tabs to align columns, you won't experience an attack of the "wavies."*

Default tab stops are set left-aligned every .5". The tabs are visible on the ruler as small upside down "Ts".

Default tab stop every 0.5"

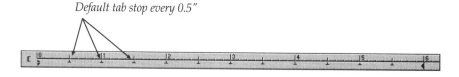

Word for Windows has four types of tab alignment:

- Left
- Center
- Right
- Decimal

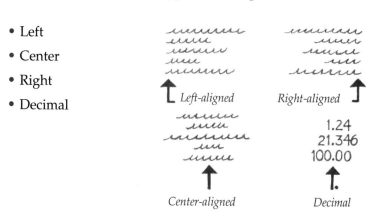

Left-aligned   *Right-aligned*

1.24
21.346
100.00

Center-aligned   *Decimal*

It'll be easier to learn how to create and change tabs on a blank screen, so choose New from the File menu and click OK to accept the Normal template.

There are two schools of thought when it comes to creating a table using tabs. One is to set the tab stops first and then type the text. The other is to type the text and tabs first, highlight the block, and then set the tab stops at the desired locations. In this exercise, you'll use the first method. As with other features of Word for Windows, there are many ways to get the same result. The correct way to do it is the way you feel most comfortable.

How to Set Tab Stops

You can set tab stops using the Tabs dialog box or the ribbon. In the next sections, you'll try both methods, and then you'll type a table using the tab stops you've set.

Using the Tabs Dialog Box to Set Tab Stops

To practice setting tab stops using the Tabs dialog box, follow these steps:

1. Choose Tabs from the Format menu. The Tabs dialog box appears.

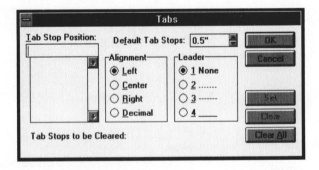

2. Select the type of alignment. In this case, left alignment is already selected, so leave it that way.

3. Type **.75** in the Tab Stop Position box and click OK.

Notice the left-aligned tab at the 3/4" mark on the ruler.

Using the Ribbon to Set Tab Stops

As you'll remember, the ribbon is located just above the ruler. On the far-right side of the ribbon are icons representing the four types of tabs. (Other items on the ribbon are covered in Chapter 10.)

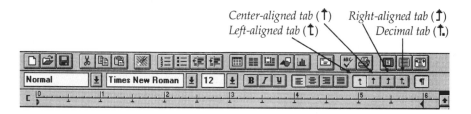

Center-aligned tab (↑)   Right-aligned tab (↑)
Left-aligned tab (↑)   Decimal tab (↑.)

To set a tab stop using the ribbon, click the icon of the desired tab type, then click the ruler where you want the tab stop to be set.

Note: *You must click the bottom half of the ruler to set the tab stop. Clicking the row with the ruler numbers does not set tab stops.*

To practice using the ribbon, set the following tab stops:

- Center tab at 2"
- Right tab at 3.75"
- Decimal tab at 5"

Now that the tab stops are set, let's type the table. Because you set four tab stops, you will press TAB four times within each line, and then press ENTER to go to the next line.

For the first line of the table:

1. Press TAB, and type **Year**.
2. Press TAB, and type **Manufacturer**.

3. Press TAB, and type **Model**.

4. Press TAB, and type **Price**.

5. Press ENTER to go to the next line.

Using this model for typing the text, finish entering the table.

Year	Manufacturer	Model	Price
1965	General Motors	Cadillac	$4,000.00
1990	Toyota	Camry	$14,000.00
1989	Acura	Legend	$20,000.00
1992	Mercedes	500SL	$79,000.00
1978	Plymouth	Horizon	$1,500.00

Note: *The only time you should press* SPACEBAR *is to separate words within a column, such as "General Motors."*

When you are done, you'll see the table onscreen with the first column left aligned, the second column center aligned, the third column right aligned, and the last column decimal aligned.

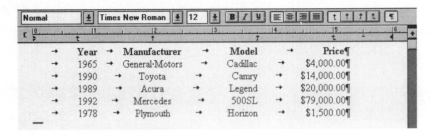

How to Move Tab Stops

Sometimes you may need to move tab stops. For example, you might create a table and then decide that one column is too close to another. You would then need to move the tab setting for that column so that there would be more space between columns.

When moving tab stops, it is *very important* to highlight all the lines of the table (and not the lines immediately above or below the table) before you adjust the tab positions on the ruler. If you do not highlight the table, you change the tab settings for only the line where the cursor is sitting.

The quickest way to move tab stops is to drag the tabs on the ruler to new positions. To practice, follow these steps:

1. Highlight all six lines of the table.
2. Drag the left tab to .5". Notice that all the first-column items move together.
3. Drag the center tab to 1.75".
4. Drag the right tab to 3.5".
5. Drag the decimal tab to 4.75".
6. Click in the text area to see the changes.

Notice that the word *Price* is really not properly aligned with the numbers in the column. On your screen, the top line is not in boldface either. For practice, change the tab position in just the first line and make the entire line bold so it stands out from the rest:

1. Highlight the entire top line of the sample table.
2. Press CTRL-B to make the line bold.
3. Drag the decimal tab to just short of the 5" mark.

The table is now ready for you to print. After printing, save the document as TABLE.DOC.

How to Remove Tab Settings

To remove a tab setting from an entire table:

1. Highlight the table.
2. Drag the tab off the ruler and release the mouse.

What Do They Mean By...?

Paragraph   A line or several lines of text that ends when you press ENTER.

Paragraph Symbol   A non-printing symbol that tells Word for Windows where a paragraph ends. It contains all the formatting for that paragraph.

Paragraph Indentation   Adjusting the paragraph's location a fixed amount relative to the left and right margins.

Paragraph Alignment   How a paragraph is situated between the left and right margins. For example, a paragraph can be left aligned, right aligned, centered, or justified.

Line Spacing   The amount of blank space for the area above or below a paragraph, or between the lines in a paragraph.

Working with the Whole Document

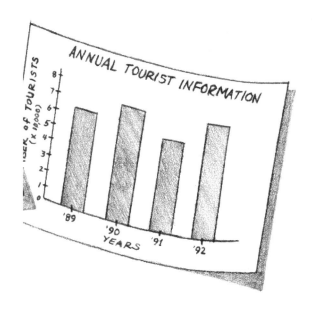

ANNUAL TOURIST INFORMATION

NUMBER OF TOURISTS (× 10,000)

YEARS

'89   '90   '91   '92

The previous two chapters discuss changing the look of small amounts of text, such as words or paragraphs. Sometimes you need to make modifications that affect larger portions of text, like a page, several pages, or even the entire file. Document formatting allows you to control several items which affect your final printed output. These items include:

- Margins
- Paper size and orientation
- Paper Source
- Page breaks
- Page numbering
- The Find and Replace commands

Margins are measurements indicating the distance from the edge of the paper to where text is to be shown. Word for Windows creates left, right, top, and bottom margins.

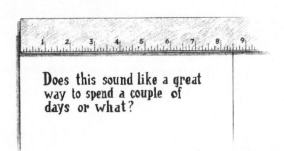

Does this sound like a great way to spend a couple of days or what?

Paper size refers to indicating the actual size of the piece of paper the document prints on. *Orientation* indicates whether the file is printed with the short or long edge of the paper at the top

Paper Source is a feature that allows you to specify which paper bin Word for Windows uses when printing your document. If you have only one paper tray, this feature is dimmed.

A *page break* indicates where one page ends and another page begins. Word for Windows creates them as you type, or they can be manually inserted.

Page numbers can print out at the top or bottom of each page. Word for Windows can also suppress the numbering on the first page.

The *Find* command searches the document for a word or phrase and pauses when the word is found. The *Replace* command looks for specific text and then changes that text to whatever you specify. Find and Replace can also look for text with specific formatting characteristics, like bold text, for example.

Margins

The Margins setting is found at the upper left of the Page Setup dialog box. Choose Page Setup from the Format menu to open this dialog box.

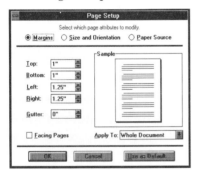

There are many reasons you might want to change the margins of your document. For example, you could increase the margins to make your document easier to read, or decrease the margins to allow more text on a page, thus reducing the length of a long document.

At the left side of the Page Setup dialog box are the Top, Bottom, Left, and Right boxes, which show the present settings for the top, bottom, left, and right margins.

There are two ways to change the margins:

- Click the change buttons next to each box.

- Highlight the current value in the margin box and type the size you want.

For practice, change the left and right margins to 1.5" and the top margin to 2". Notice the changes reflected in the Sample box.

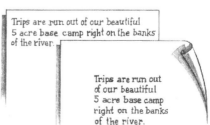

Facing Pages and Gutter

There are two options related to margins that are useful if your document is a book or long report that you are going to bind. You can specify a gutter measurement and you can have Word for Windows mirror the margins on facing pages.

If the Facing Pages check box is selected, the Left and Right margin settings become Inside and Outside. *Inside* indicates the distance of the left page's right edge of text and the right page's left edge of text from where the two pages would be bound together. *Outside* indicates the distance of the left page's left edge of text and the right page's right edge of text from the outer edges of each page. The Sample box now shows two pieces of paper. Select the Facing Pages check box to make the margins mirror each other.

INSIDE MARGIN

OUTSIDE MARGIN

The Gutter box is below the Top, Bottom, Left, and Right margin boxes. Enter a number in the Gutter box to add space to the Inside margin. For practice, leave the margin settings as set in the last example.

Then follow these steps:

1. Click the Facing Pages check box.

2. Click the change buttons next to the Gutter box to increase the gutter size to .7".

3. Note the changes in the Sample box.

4. Unselect Facing Pages and reset the gutter to 0".

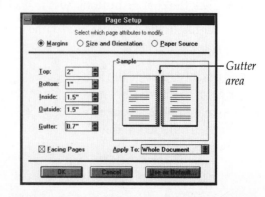

Gutter area

Apply To

The Apply To option lets you specify how much of your document will be affected by your document formatting changes. This option is located in the bottom-right corner of the Page Setup dialog box. If you click the down arrow at the right of the Apply To box, you will see a drop-down list box with two items: Whole Document and This Point Forward.

If you choose *Whole Document*, the settings you are creating affect the entire file. *This Point Forward* means these changes affect only pages from the current page on. You might

use This Point Forward, for example, if the first page of a letter is printed on letterhead paper but the rest of the letter is printed on regular paper. The first page would require a larger top margin to make room for the logo. From page two on, the top margin could be smaller.

Size and Orientation

The Size and Orientation button, at the top middle of the Page Setup dialog box, allows you to select paper size and orientation. When you click the Size and Orientation button, the Page Setup dialog box changes to reflect these options.

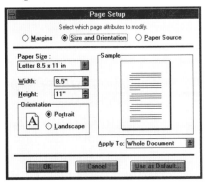

The Paper Size option allows you to choose from many different sizes of paper. You can also create a custom size by clicking the change buttons for Width and Height. Refer to the owner's manual for your printer to see the sizes of paper your printer can use.

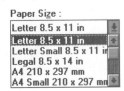

The Orientation option allows you to choose portrait or landscape orientation. *Portrait orientation* refers to a page that is taller than it is wide. In *landscape orientation,* the page is wider than it is tall. Text is normally printed in portrait orientation. Landscape is often used when creating text tables (columnar text) that are too wide to fit well in Portrait mode.

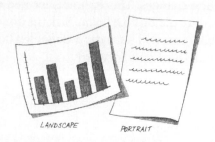

LANDSCAPE   PORTRAIT

The Apply To drop-down list box is available for Size and Orientation. This is extremely convenient if you need a page or two in the middle of a document to be printed in landscape orientation (a chart or wide table of figures, for example) but the rest of the file printed in portrait orientation.

Paper Source

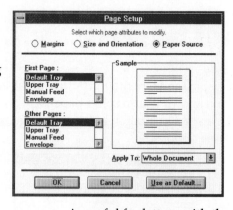

The *Paper Source* option, at the top right of the Page Setup dialog box, allows you to use different paper bins on your printer. If your printer has more than one source to feed paper, you can specify which bin Word for Windows uses for the first page and for other pages. This option

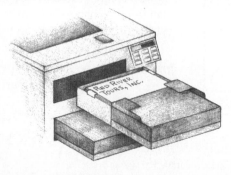

is useful for letters with the first page on letterhead and subsequent pages on regular paper. (If you do not have multiple paper bins, this option is not applicable.) Apply To options are available in Paper Source as well.

Once you are finished exploring the different options

for Page Setup, click Cancel to negate any changes you've made and return to the document.

Page Breaks

As you type a document, Word for Windows uses your margin settings to determine how much text will fit on a page, and creates automatic page breaks accordingly. A *page break* appears as a line on the screen, marking the end of one page and the beginning of the next. The page where the cursor is located is indicated on the status bar at the bottom of the screen.

Speak to you soon,

....

Cathy

Automatic page break

Inserting Page Breaks

Speak to you soon,

....

Cathy

Manual page break

There may be occasions when you want a line of text to begin a new page. For example, you might want each new topic in a report to begin a page so that the report is easy to read. You can manually insert page breaks to force text to begin on a new page.

There are two ways to manually insert a page break:

- Press CTRL-ENTER
- Choose Break from the Insert menu

If you press CTRL-ENTER, a manual page break is inserted at the cursor location. If you choose Break from the Insert menu, the Break dialog box opens.

Be sure the option button next to Page Break is selected, then click OK. Word for Windows inserts a manual page break. The other options in the Break dialog box are beyond the scope of this book; see your Word for Windows user's guide for instructions on how to use them.

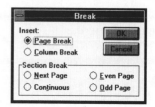

Tip: Manual page breaks can be highlighted and deleted just like any other character. To highlight a manual page break, move the pointer in the selection area next to the page break, and click. Once it is selected, press DEL *to delete it.*

For practice, open the RAFTING2.DOC file, and follow these steps:

1. Position the cursor on the line above "Unlike most other rivers."
2. Insert a manual page break.
3. Choose Print Preview from the File menu.
4. Click Two Pages to preview both pages.
5. Click Cancel to return to the document.

Page Numbering

Word for Windows can automatically insert page numbers at the top or bottom of every page. Printed page numbers are often helpful to the reader. You can choose to have text included with the number ("Budget Report Page 3" or "Page 4 of 15") or just the number. Word for Windows also offers an option that prevents page numbers from appearing on the first page.

There are two methods to add page numbers:

- Choose Page Numbers from the Insert menu.
- Choose Header/Footer from the View menu.

Page Numbers

The Page Numbers command inserts just a page number and does not allow the inclusion of text. By design, the Page Number command puts the page number on all pages except the first page (standard business format usually omits a page number on the first page). If you want to include text along with the page number or have a page number appear on the first page, use the Header/Footer command, discussed later in this section.

Note: View the options in the dialog boxes shown next to see what's available, but click Cancel when finished. Exercises for adding page numbers follow in the "Header/Footer" section.

Choose Page Numbers from the Insert menu. The Page Numbers dialog box appears:

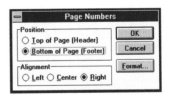

The Position option allows you to specify whether the page number appears at the top or bottom of the page.

The number can appear left-, center-, or right-aligned. These options can be selected under Alignment.

Click the Format button, and the Page Number Format dialog box appears.

The Page Number Format dialog box gives the following choices:

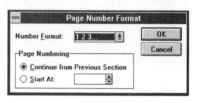

- Number Format

- Continue from Previous Section

- Start At

The Number Format option lets you specify a page number style for your document. Click the down arrow next to the Number Format box. A drop-down list box appears with the following options:

- Arabic numerals (1 2 3...)

- Lowercase letters (a b c...)

- Uppercase letters (A B C...)

- Lowercase Roman numerals (i ii iii...)

- Uppercase Roman numerals (I II III...)

Click your desired page number format.

The Continue from Previous Section option keeps the numbering consecutive from a previous section (if the document has been divided into sections). For further information about sections, take a look at your Word for Windows user's guide.

The Start At option lets you specify the starting number to print on the first page of the document. Click the change buttons to increase or decrease the number. If, for example, you set the number to 3, Word for Windows prints a 3 on the first page of the file, a 4 on the second page, and so on. The Start At feature can be useful if you have two separate files that you wish to have numbered consecutively. For example, if the first file ends on page 15, the second document can be set to start page numbering at 16.

After exploring the dialog boxes for Insert Page Number, click twice on Cancel to return to the document.

Header/Footer

A *header* is text that appears at the top of every page when the file is printed. A *footer* is text that appears at the bottom of every page when the file is printed. Headers and footers can contain page numbers, the date and time you print the file, or any other text you want. Choose Header/Footer

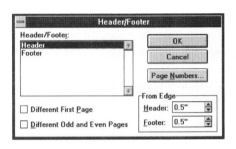

from the View menu, and the Header/Footer dialog box appears.

The From Edge option, at the bottom-right of the dialog box, allows you to change the distance between the top edge of the page and the header, as well as the distance from the bottom of the page to the footer.

The Page Numbers button opens the same dialog box as the Page Number command. It allows you to choose the page number style for the document.

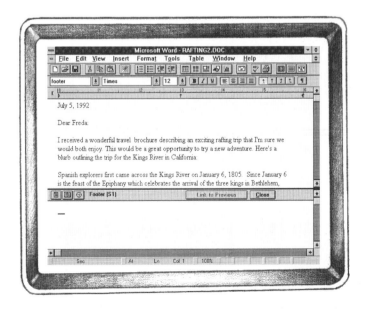

To type text for a header or footer, click Header or Footer in the Header/Footer box in the upper-left corner, and click OK. A Header or Footer window opens that gives you space to type in your text.

The window has its own vertical scroll bar, as well as a split screen bar separating the text pane from the Header/Footer pane.

To close the Header/Footer window, do one of the following:

- Click the Close button

- Double-click the split screen bar

- Drag the split screen bar to the top or bottom of the main document scroll bar and release the mouse button

Header/Footer Buttons

There are five buttons across the top of the Header/Footer pane.

The first button inserts the Page Number into the header or footer. This is an alternate way of inserting page numbers, if you didn't use the Page Number command from the Insert menu.

The second button adds the current date to the header or footer.

The third button adds the current time to the header or footer. Word for Windows reads the date of the internal clock of your computer, if it has one.

Note: The date and time buttons insert the current date and time when you print. For example, if you create a file on July 10 at 10 A.M. and use the date or time button, then print the file on August 3 at 9:45 P.M., the August date and time are printed. If you want the original date to print, type the date as text and do not use the date or time button.

The fourth button links the header or footer text in successive sections of multiple-section documents.

The last button closes the window.

Tip: The Header/Footer window can also be closed by double-clicking the split screen bar that separates the two windows.

With RAFTING2.DOC still open, try these steps for practice:

1. With the Footer pane visible, press TAB once, then type **Page** and press SPACEBAR.

2. Click the Page Number button.

3. Highlight "Page 1," make it bold, and enlarge the character size to 18-point. (Take a look at Chapter 7 for how to change character formats.)

   To see what the document looks like, choose Print Preview from the File menu. Your preview should look like this:

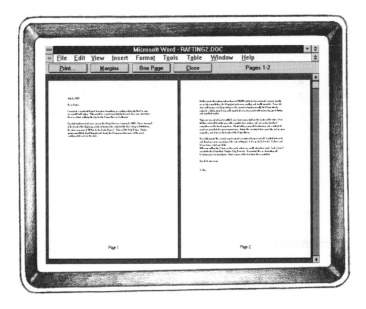

4. Click Close to exit from Preview.

5. Close the Footer window if it hasn't been closed.

Multiple Headers and Footers

In standard business documents, the first page generally does not include a page number, or it might have different header or footer text than the rest of the file. Word for Windows can create a separate header and footer for the first page. Books also sometimes have different headers and footers for odd- and even-numbered pages. Word for Windows takes care of that as well.

To create multiple headers and footers:

1. Choose Headers/Footers from the View menu.

2. When the Header/Footer dialog box appears, click the Different First Page check box. The Header/Footer list changes slightly to add two new items.

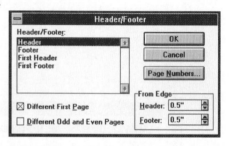

You now have the ability to create a first header or first footer. Click the desired option and create the first header or first footer the same way you create a regular header or footer.

Odd and Even Headers or Footers

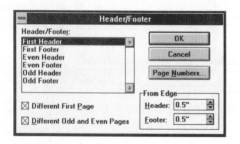

If you want to create different headers or footers for odd and even pages of your document, click the Different Odd and Even Pages check box. The regular Header and Footer entries are replaced with Even Header, Even Footer, Odd Header, and Odd Footer.

To create an odd and even header and footer, choose Header/Footer from the View menu and click the check box for Different Odd and Even Pages.

For practice:

1. Select the check box for Different First Page.

2. Double-click on First Footer. The First Footer window should be blank because Word for Windows assumes you want something different from the Footer.

3. Leave it blank to assure no page number appears on page one.

4. Click Close.

5. Choose Print Preview from the File menu and view the results.

The preview now shows page one without a page number, but page two's footer text remains.

6. Click Cancel to exit from Print Preview.

Find

The Find command searches a document for a specified word or phrase. It also allows you to look for text that has been formatted a certain way or that is a specific case.

The Find command can be useful if, for example, you know you have made a reference to Ms. Davis somewhere in your file but have forgotten what page it is on. Using Find, you can jump the cursor to that text.

Position the cursor at the beginning of RAFTING2.DOC and choose Find from the Edit menu. The Find dialog box opens.

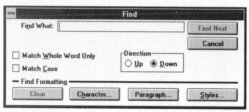

The Find What box is where you enter the text you need to find. The Direction option buttons allow the search to go from the cursor position up to the beginning of the file, or down to the end of the file. If the cursor is in the middle of the file, and you choose to search from that point to the end of the file, you see a dialog box when Find reaches the end of the file. This dialog box asks if you want to continue searching at the beginning.

If you choose instead to search from the middle of the file up to the beginning of the file, the dialog box asks you if you want to continue searching at the end.

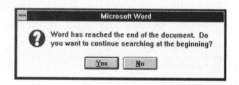

Clicking the Find Next button starts the search for the word in the Find What box. If the word is found, it is highlighted within the document. If this is the occurrence of the word you were looking for, click on Cancel to close the Find dialog box. If you need to look further, click Find Next again and the search continues.

The Match Whole Word Only check box makes Find locate the exact word or phrase. For example, if you are looking for the word *sense*, selecting Match Whole Word Only prevents Find from stopping on words such as *nonsense* or *senseless*.

The Match Case check box causes Find to stop only if the case of the word or phrase matches that in the Find What box. For example, if you typed *Kings* in the Find What box, Find would not stop at *kings* or *KINGS*.

Character allows you to focus the search on a word or phrase that has been formatted differently from the other occurrences. This dialog box is virtually identical to the one viewed when choosing Character from the

Format menu. Turn to Chapter 7 for more information about the items in this dialog box.

Paragraph allows you to narrow the search to text with a specific paragraph format. If, for example, the word or phrase is within a center-aligned paragraph, Find stops only at those occurrences.

For practice:

1. Choose Find from the Edit menu.

2. Type **kings** in the Find What box and click Match Case.

3. Click Character, and the Find Character dialog box appears.

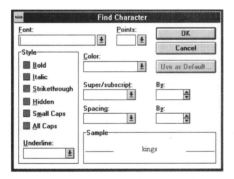

4. Click the gray box next to Bold and Italic in the Style area. Click OK. This returns you to the Find dialog box. Notice the words Bold Italic next to Format. Only the word *kings* in bold and italic will be found.

5. Click Paragraph. The Find Paragraph dialog box appears.

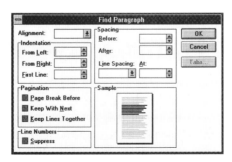

6. Click the down arrow next to the Alignment box in the upper-left corner. Choose Centered from the drop-down list box, and click OK.

Centered has been added in the Format line in the Find dialog box. Only a bold, italic, and center-aligned *kings* will be found.

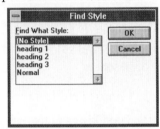

7. Click Styles.

The Find dialog box opens. It shows the styles available with the document.

8. Click Normal and click OK. Notice the changes in the Find dialog box. This time, only normal-styled, bold, italic, and center-aligned *kings* will be found.

If you made a mistake with one of the choices, click the appropriate button, make the changes, and return to the Find dialog box

9. Click Clear.

The Clear button removes any special formatting requests from the search.

10. Click Find Next. Word for Windows stops at the word *kings* on the second line in the second paragraph.

If this was not the particular occurrence you were searching for, clicking Find Next moves to the next time the word or phrase appears.

11. Click Find Next again. Since lowercase *kings* is in the file only once, a message appears telling you that you've reached the end of the document.

The message indicates that you have seen all occurrences of the item searched for from the original cursor position to the end of the document. If the search was up the file, the dialog box would indicate that Find has reached the beginning of the document.

12. Click OK to respond to this message, then click Cancel to return to the file, and move the cursor to the beginning of the document.

Replace

The Replace command searches for and replaces specified text and formatting. You can confirm each time text is going to be changed or let Word for Windows change every occurrence automatically. Choose Replace from the Edit menu, and the Replace dialog box appears.

Note: *If a block of text is selected prior to choosing this command, then Replace works only within that block. The dialog box stays open after the replacements have been made. You need to click the Cancel button to return to the file.*

Because Find and Replace are closely linked in function, the last text typed in Find What from the Find command appears in Find What in the Replace command.

The same features found in the Find command for Match Whole Word Only, Match Case, Clear, Character, Paragraph, and Styles are available to make replacing specific text more precise.

To practice using the Replace command, let's replace the word *kings* with *American*:

1. Make sure the cursor is located at the beginning of RAFT-ING2.DOC, and choose Replace from the Edit menu.

2. Type **kings** in the Find What box if it's not entered already, and deactivate Match Case if necessary to make the replace case insensitive.

3. Click the Replace With box and type **American.**

4. Click the Character button, select Bold, and click OK.

5. Click Find Next. Word for Windows stops at the end of the first paragraph, with *Kings* selected. Click Replace.

6. The first change is made and you move to the next occurrence. Click replace for the next occurrence as well.

7. You now stop at the phrase "arrival of the three *kings.*" Since this word does not refer to the river name, click Find Next to move on. The word is left untouched.

8. Click Find Next when you pause at "River of Holy Kings."

9. Click Replace for all further occurrences of *Kings.* When Replace moves back to the top of the file, click Cancel.

Now let's try a global replace, where Word for Windows changes every occurrence automatically:

1. Position the cursor at the beginning of the file and choose Replace from the Edit menu.

2. Type **January 6** in the Find What box.

3. Click the Replace With box and type **July 4.**

4. Click the Character button, select Bold, and click OK.

5. Click Replace All. The two occurrences of the date change to July 4 in bold.

6. Click Close.

7. Choose Close from the File menu and click No so you don't save any changes.

What Do They Mean By...?

Margins   Measurements indicating the distance from the edge of the paper to where text is to be shown. Word for Windows creates left, right, top, and bottom margins.

Orientation   Indicates whether the file is printed with the short or long edge of the paper at the top of the page. Portrait orientation has the short edge of the paper at the top, and landscape orientation has the long edge at the top.

Automatic page break   A page break that Word for Windows creates when text and graphics can't fit on the current page.

Manual page break   A page break you generate to force certain text and graphics to be on a specific page.

Header   Text of one or more lines that appears at the top of each page, above the document text.

Footer   Text of one or more lines that appears at the bottom of each page, below the text of the document.

Find   A command that locates specified words, phrases, or formatting.

Replace   A command that locates and changes specific words, phrases, or formatting.

Using the Toolbar and the Ribbon

10

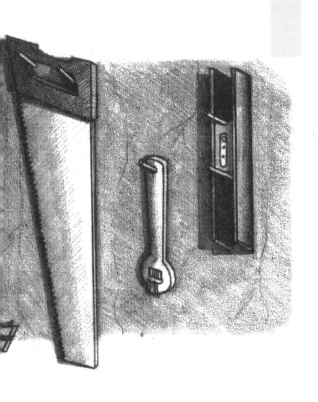

A section in Chapter 8 describes how to set tab stops by choosing Tabs from the Format menu. You can also set tab stops by selecting a tab type from the ribbon, and then clicking the desired placement on the ruler.

In Chapter 3 you learned that to print a document, you can choose Print from the File menu. You can also print by clicking the Printer button on the toolbar.

Many commands found in various dialog boxes are also items on the ribbon and the toolbar. To choose an item, just click it. This means that with Word for Windows, you have at least two ways to perform certain functions—either open a menu or click an item on the toolbar or ribbon. You choose which is the best way for you.

The toolbar is located directly below the the menu bar, and the ribbon is below the toolbar.

Toolbar  *Ribbon*

To hide or show either the toolbar or ribbon, open the View menu. If a checkmark appears next to the toolbar, ribbon, or ruler item on the menu, it is showing onscreen. If checkmarks aren't showing and you want to make an item visible, select the item you wish to appear. To follow along in this chapter, make the toolbar, ribbon, and ruler visible.

Using the Toolbar

This section explains how to use all of the buttons on the toolbar. Many of the features mentioned here are covered in greater detail in other chapters, where they are accessed through the menu system. The new features in this chapter are:

- Applying Styles
- Bulleted List
- Envelope

- Microsoft Draw
- Microsoft Graph
- Numbered List
- Tables
- Text Columns
- Zoom 100 Percent
- Zoom Page Width
- Zoom Whole Page

New

The New button opens a new document in the Normal template. Clicking this button is the equivalent of choosing New from the File menu, choosing the Normal template, and clicking OK.

Open

The Open button on the toolbar and the Open command from the File menu give you the same dialog box. From there, you can open an existing file for editing and printing.

Save

The Save button saves the active document under its current name. If you are saving a file for the first time, the Save As dialog box appears.

Cut

The Cut button performs the same operation as choosing Cut from the Edit menu. Any selected text is stored on the Clipboard.

Copy

The Copy button performs the same operation as choosing Copy from the Edit menu. As with the Cut command, any highlighted words or graphics are stored on the Clipboard.

Paste

The Paste button works the same as choosing the Paste command from the Edit menu. Items on the Clipboard are inserted at the cursor position.

Undo

The Undo button reverses the last action. Be aware that some actions cannot be undone. For example, the Save command can't be "unsaved."

Numbered List

The Numbered List button takes selected paragraphs and sequentially numbers them. At the same time, this command creates a hanging indent so the text of the paragraph is indented 1/4-inch from the number. The numbers are Arabic numerals (1, 2, 3...).

Clicking the Numbered List button is a quick way to set up several paragraphs that need to be numbered. The manual way to accomplish this is to type the numbers in front of each paragraph, highlight the paragraphs, then set the indent on the ruler.

For practice:

1. Open the RAFTING2.DOC file and select the first three paragraphs.

2. Click the Numbered List button. The text should look like the following:

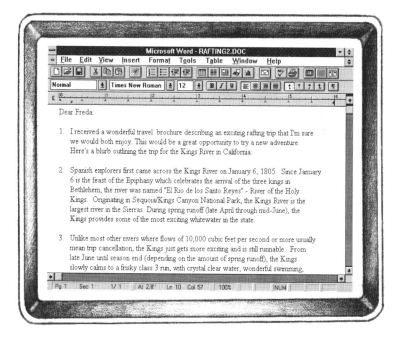

3. Click the Undo button.

Note: Choosing Undo from the Edit menu or clicking the Undo button on the toolbar returns the paragraphs to their original format, but only if you haven't made any other changes to your document in the meantime. If you use the Numbered List button, go on to other tasks, and then wish to change the format of the paragraphs, you will have to manually erase the numbers and change the indents.

Bulleted List

 The Bulleted List button works similarly to the Numbered List button, except a bullet appears at the beginning of the selected paragraphs instead of a number.

Unindent

 The Unindent button moves the selected paragraphs left to the previous tab stop. You can also use the CTRL-M keyboard equivalent.

Indent

 The Indent button moves the selected paragraphs to the right, to the next tab stop. The keyboard equivalent for this button is CTRL-N.

Table

 The Table button inserts a table at the cursor position. A *table* is a series of boxes, called cells, that are arranged in columns and rows. The width of the columns can be adjusted, and the height of the rows automatically changes according to the amount of text you type within a cell. Tables are an alternative to using tabs to set up columnar text.

When you click the Table button, a grid appears below the button. Drag the mouse to specify how many rows and columns you want to create. When you release the mouse, the table is incorporated into the document. To create a table using the Table button:

1. Move the cursor where you want the table to be inserted.

2. Click the Table button and drag the mouse down into the grid that appears beneath the Table button.
   The size of the table is indicated by how many white squares you drag over and darken. The dimensions, in rows and columns, of the table are shown at the bottom of the grid.

3. Release the mouse when the table is the desired size.

The cursor is now in the upper-left cell in the table. To create a table through the menu system, choose Insert Table from the Table menu. For more information about tables, see the Word for Windows user's guide.

Text Columns

The Text Columns button formats the document into one or more *Newspaper-style columns* (also called snaking columns) which flow text from the bottom of one column to the top of the next. This is often used when creating newsletters. When you click the Text Columns button, a picture of six columns appears.

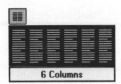

You can format your document into one to six columns by dragging the mouse. For a quick look at how the Text Columns button works, follow these steps:

1. Change RAFTING2.DOC to two-column format. It appears that the text takes up only the left half of the screen.

2. Choose Print Preview from the File menu to get a better idea of what the file will look like when printed.

3. Return the file to single-column format by clicking the Text Columns button, dragging the highlight back to one column, then releasing the mouse.

To create a multiple column document:

1. Position the mouse on the Text column button.

2. Hold down the mouse button and drag over the white columns. The number of columns is indicated by how many columns you darken. You can create up to six columns.

3. Release the mouse once you have darkened the desired number of columns.

Your document will instantly change to a multicolumn file.

Frame

The Frame button puts a non-printing *frame,* or box, around selected text or graphics, or it inserts a blank frame where you can type text or insert a graphic. You can move the frame anywhere on the page, and the document text wraps around it. Frames are very useful when used in conjunction with text columns. You can take a framed graphic and insert it, for example, between two columns.

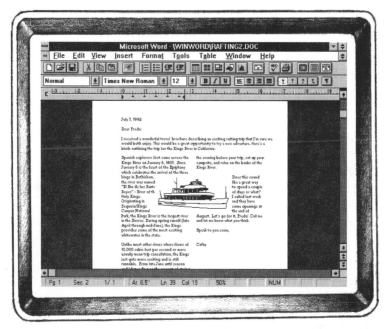

You can read more about frames in the Word for Windows user's guide.

Draw

The Draw button starts the Microsoft Draw program. Microsoft Draw is called an embedded application. *Embedded applications* work from inside other applications. They cannot be started up by themselves.

With the tools it provides, Microsoft Draw allows you to draw your own art or import drawings created in other programs. Graphics are covered in Chapter 13.

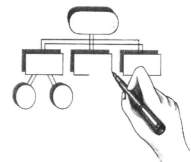

Note: If you did not install Microsoft Draw when you installed Word for Windows, clicking the Draw button does nothing.

Graph

The Graph button opens up Microsoft Graph, another embedded program that comes with Word for Windows. The Graph program allows you to create charts that can be placed in your document. Clicking the Graph button on the toolbar opens the Microsoft Graph window, along with a sample chart. The names of the two windows reflect the name of the file you are working on at the time you click the Graph button.

Refer to the Microsoft Graph book provided with Word for Windows for more details.

Note: If you did not install Microsoft Graph when you installed Word for Windows, clicking the Graph button does nothing.

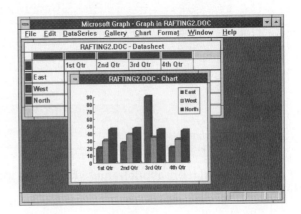

Envelope

The Envelope button allows you to create an envelope that prints along with your document.

Note: *Your printer must be able to accept manually fed paper and envelopes for you to print envelopes. Check the owner's manual for your printer for this information.*

When you click the Envelope button, the Create Envelope dialog box appears.

Caution: Be sure your cursor is at the beginning of the file when you select the Envelope button. If you are in the middle of the file, some of the document text might be accidentally included with the envelope text.

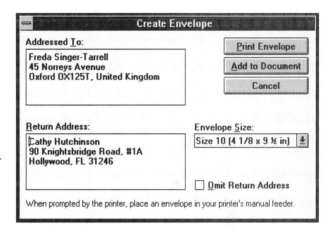

The box in the upper-left corner is for the person who will receive the letter. The bottom-left box is for the return address. The return address is automatically entered in the bottom-left box based on information you entered when you installed Word for Windows. You can edit this text as desired.

You can select the Omit Return Address check box in the lower-right corner of the dialog box to prevent printing the return address. Click this box if your envelope has your return address preprinted.

Click the down arrow next to the Envelope Size box to open a drop-down list box that specifies the different-sized envelopes Word for Windows can work with. You can select the envelope size you want from this list.

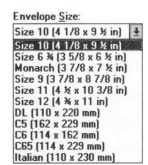

The Print Envelope command button sends the envelope print job to the printer.

The Add to Document command button adds the envelope information to the active document. This step allows you to print the envelope at any time instead of having to retype the address. A separate page in the shape of an envelope is added to the file. If you save the file with the envelope page inserted, then the next time you open the file, the envelope page is the first page of the file, followed by the document.

Spelling

The Spelling button starts the Word for Windows spell checking feature. Clicking this button is equivalent to choosing Spelling from the Tools menu. Spelling scans your document, pauses at words it doesn't know, and offers suggestions for the correct spelling. This topic is covered in more detail in Chapter 11.

Print

The Print button starts printing the active file. It prints one copy of the full document. Alternatively, you can use the Print command from the File menu, which opens a dialog box with several options.

Zoom Whole Page

The Zoom Whole Page button displays an entire page onscreen. It is similar to Print Preview, but you can edit your text from this view. This feature is helpful if you are creating newsletters and brochures, which often use large text for headlines, and you want to get a bird's-eye view of the file.

Zoom 100 Percent

If you have clicked either the Zoom Whole Page or Zoom Page Width button or used the Zoom command to change to another size view, the Zoom 100 Percent button returns you to normal, actual-size view.

Zoom Page Width

The Zoom Page Width button is helpful if you change the size of the left and right margins. Zoom Page Width adjusts the view so you can see all text from margin to margin across the screen.

Compare the view of RAFTING2.DOC when the margins are 2" on both sides and when they are .5" on both sides. Here is the file with 2" left and right margins, after clicking Zoom Page Width:

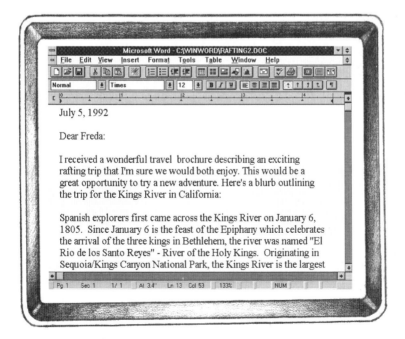

There is 4.5" of typing space on a piece of paper that is 8.5" wide. Notice that the screen stretches to show only up to the 4.5" mark on the ruler.

Here is RAFTING2.DOC with .5" margins, after clicking Zoom Page Width:

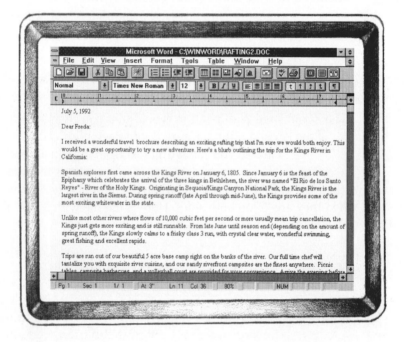

Now there is 7.5 inches of typing space. The Zoom Page Width button causes the type to shrink onscreen to accommodate all the text. Normal view would hide the right edge of text when you are not viewing it, which can be awkward when typing.

Using the Ribbon

The ribbon makes text formatting faster and more convenient. To use the ribbon, select the desired text, then click the appropriate button or open a drop-down list box and select the desired option.

The settings on the ribbon indicate the format currently applied to the document. For example, if your cursor is on text that is formatted as 12-point Times, the Font box on the ribbon will read "Times," and the Point size box will read "12." If you move your cursor to a part of the document with a different format, the ribbon indicates the settings in effect for that part.

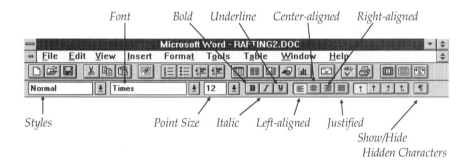

Applying Styles

The first item on the ribbon is the Styles box. You click the down arrow to the right of the box to open a drop-down list box of styles you can apply to selected paragraphs. A style is a group of character and paragraph formats that you assign a name. Styles make consistent formatting much quicker.

For example, assume the subject headings of a report need to be bold, underlined, 14-point Times New Roman font, with 12 points of extra spacing above and below the text. You could type the subject heading, select the text, make all the changes, and move on to the next subject heading and repeat the process. However, if you created a style called heading 1 that contained all the above format characteristics, you could type the text, apply the heading 1 style, and Word for Windows would make all the format changes at once. Take a look at your Word for Windows documentation for more information about styles.

Applying Fonts

The second item on the ribbon is the Font box. You can open the drop-down list box to show the available fonts. Select the desired font from this list. This is the same list that appears in the Character dialog box.

Applying Point Sizes

The Point Size box is the next item on the ribbon. Open the drop-down list box to show all the point sizes available, from 4 points to 127 points, in one-point increments.

If you wish to use a point size not showing in the drop-down list, such as 16.5:

1. Select the text you wish to change.
2. Drag across the number in the Point Size box.
3. Press the DEL or BACKSPACE key to erase the number in the box.
4. Type in the desired number, in this case **16.5**, and press ENTER.

Applying Character Formats

The next three buttons on the ribbon create bold, italic, and single underline formatting. First select the desired text, then click the appropriate button.

Tip: If you need to use a different underline style, choose Character from the Format menu instead.

If you wish to reverse the formatting action of these buttons, click the buttons again and the formatting reverts to normal. For more information about character formats, turn to Chapter 7.

Applying Paragraph Formats

 The four Alignment buttons on the ribbon create left-aligned, center-aligned, right-aligned, and justified paragraphs. If you wish to change the alignment of one paragraph, place the cursor anywhere in the paragraph and click the desired alignment button. If you need to change the alignment of more than a single paragraph at one time, select the paragraphs first, then click the appropriate alignment button. For more information about paragraph alignment, turn to Chapter 8.

Setting Tab Stops

The four Tab buttons on the ribbon are used to set left, center, right, and decimal tab stops on the ruler. Chapter 8 discusses how to set tab stops using the ribbon.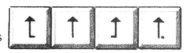

Show/Hide Hidden Characters

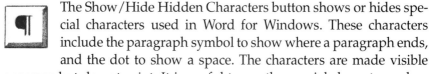 The Show/Hide Hidden Characters button shows or hides special characters used in Word for Windows. These characters include the paragraph symbol to show where a paragraph ends, and the dot to show a space. The characters are made visible onscreen but do not print. It is useful to see the special characters when you are verifying document formatting. The next screen is a screen with Hidden Characters showing.

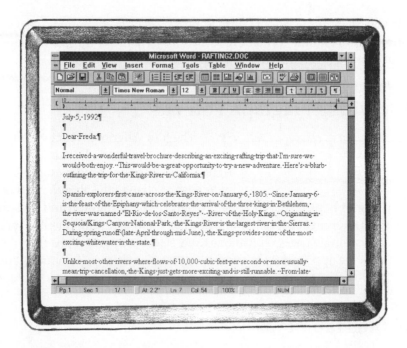

What Do They Mean By...?

Toolbar   A part of the Word for Windows screen that gives quick access to some of the most frequently used commands.

Ribbon   A part of the Word for Windows screen located just below the toolbar. The buttons on the ribbon allow you to quickly perform frequently used character and paragraph formatting commands.

Finishing Touches —Spelling and Thesaurus

11

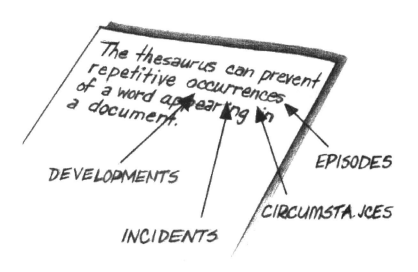

The thesaurus can prevent repetitive occurrences of a word appearing in a document.

DEVELOPMENTS

EPISODES

CIRCUMSTANCES

INCIDENTS

This chapter covers two word processing features that have made writing letters by hand as old-fashioned as the icebox. The *Spelling* feature corrects the spelling of the document. Spelling pauses at words it doesn't recognize and, in many cases, offers suggestions for the correct spelling. The *Thesaurus* looks at a word you specify and gives *synonyms* (words that have the same or nearly the same meaning), as well as *antonyms* (words with the opposite meaning). Some words can have more than one meaning, such as the word *test*. Since *test* can be either a noun or a verb, the Thesaurus shows its alternate meanings.

If you have never misspelled a word and you know several synonyms for each word you write, you might never need to read this chapter. It might be a good idea, though, to at least check the spelling of your work, to be sure your accurate eye didn't miss something. Also, how many times can you use the same word in one paragraph? Maybe the Thesaurus can provide a similar word that conveys the same thought.

Note: If you did not install the Thesaurus feature when you installed Word for Windows, you will not be able to follow along for that part of the lesson. If you wish to install Thesaurus, refer to the Word for Windows user's guide.

Spelling

The Spelling feature built into Word for Windows comes with its own dictionary, which contains more than 100,000 words. You can create an unlimited number of custom dictionaries, adding an additional 10,000 words to each custom dictionary. The kinds of words

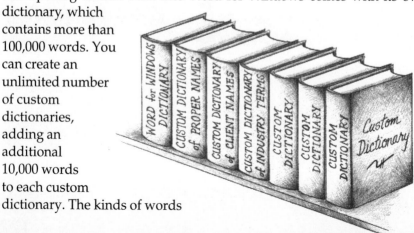

you might want to add are proper names, product codes, client names, or terms that are specific to the industry in which you work.

Spelling not only stops at words that aren't in the dictionary, it also pauses at double words, such as *the the,* and asks if you wish to delete one of the words. Unusual capitalization, such as WINdows, also causes Spelling to pause. Spelling checks the entire document unless you select a block of text before issuing the Spelling command.

Using Spelling

To practice using Spelling, open the file named RAFTING2.DOC. Type **the** after the first *the* in the last sentence of the second paragraph. This will show you what Spelling does when it encounters double words. After typing, position the cursor at the beginning of the file.

You can start Spelling one of two ways:

- Click the Spelling button on the toolbar

- Choose Spelling from the Tools menu

Either command opens the Spelling dialog box.

Spelling stops at the first word it doesn't understand, which in this case is the proper name Freda.

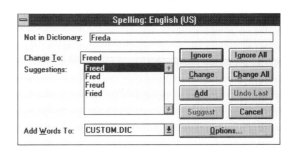

You have several options at this point:

- If you agree with the suggestion in the Change To box, click the Change button.

- If you wish to enter your own replacement, delete the word in the Change To box, type in the replacement word, and then click the Change button.

- If you want to replace the word with one in the Suggestions box, click that word, then click the Change button.

Change

Clicking Change for any of these preceding options makes the change for this one occurrence only. If Spelling encounters the word again in the file, it pauses once more and asks you to correct it again.

Change All

Change All searches the entire document and changes each occurrence to the word in the Change To box.

Ignore

The Ignore button tells Spelling to skip this occurrence of the word. If Spelling encounters the word again in the file, it pauses once more.

Ignore All

Ignore All tells Spelling to skip any further occurrences of that word.

Add

The Add button adds the word to the custom dictionary listed in the Add Words To box. You could start a custom dictionary that includes business terms, friend's names, or any words that you expect to use frequently.

Note: Spelling will not pause at words that are used incorrectly. For example, in the sentence, "She through the ball across the field," "through" is a correctly spelled word, but the proper word is "threw." To catch these usage errors, refer to the Grammar feature in your Word for Windows user's guide.

Once you have made any of these choices, Spelling moves to the next word it doesn't recognize. In this case, click Ignore to continue.

Spelling stops next at *los*, thinking there's an error in capitalization, and asks if *los* should be *Los*. Click Ignore to move on. Click Ignore again to pass *Reyes*.

The next stop is *the the*. Click the Delete button, and Spelling deletes one of the duplicate words.

Spelling next pauses at *whitewater* and suggests that the word should be split into two words, *white water*. Since *whitewater* is a term used in the rafting industry, it does not need to be corrected. Click Ignore.

Continue checking the rest of the document and respond appropriately when Spelling pauses.

Note: *The Undo Last button undoes the last five corrections, one at a time. Clicking once undoes the most recent correction, a second click undoes the second most recent correction, and so on.*

When Spelling is finished, a dialog box alerts you. Click OK to return to the document.

If your cursor was not at the beginning of the file when you issued the Spelling command, a message will ask whether you wish to have Spelling continue from the top of the file or stop at the end of the file.

Tip: *Once you have finished spell checking, it would be wise to save the document at that point to ensure an*

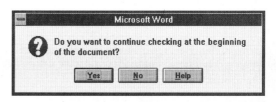

accurate file on disk. However, for this lesson, you do not need to save any changes.

Thesaurus

Another valuable tool in Word for Windows is the Thesaurus. A thesaurus looks up synonyms—words with similar meanings—for the selected word. If you ever have trouble finding just the right word or phrase, the Thesaurus can suggest a few options. Or, if you have reviewed your file and have noticed that the same word is used over and over (and over...), you might want to find alternatives. The Word for Windows Thesaurus can offer some choices. (For example, Word for Windows gives "choice" as one alternative word for "alternative!")

The Thesaurus can also present you with antonyms (words that have the opposite meaning to the selected word), as well as words that are related to the selected word. A related word is generally a word which shares the same root with the selected word. A listing of related words, for example, for "associated" would include "associate."

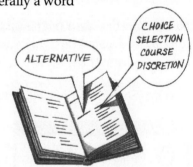

Using the Thesaurus

The Thesaurus contains 200,000 synonyms based on 24,000 keywords. A *keyword* is the word whose synonyms you want to find. For practice using the Thesaurus, open RAFTING2.DOC if it is not still open.

1. Highlight the word "exciting" in the first sentence of the first paragraph.

   Tip: If you do not select a word before issuing the Thesaurus command, Word for Windows looks up the word closest to the cursor or the word the cursor is on.

2. Choose Thesaurus from the Tools menu. The Thesaurus dialog box appears.

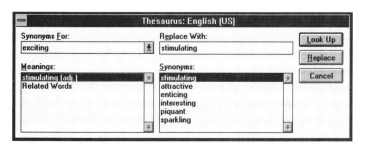

The Synonyms For box shows the keyword currently being used by the Thesaurus.

The Meanings box shows possible meanings for the selected word. The first meaning also appears in the Replace With box and the Synonyms box.

You have the following options at this point:

- To replace the keyword with a word in the Synonyms box, click the desired word, then click the Replace button.

- If there are words in the Meanings box, click one of them and then click the Look Up button to see meanings and synonyms for that word. It now becomes the keyword.

- If Related Words or Antonyms are available in the Meanings box, you can click either option. The Synonyms box then becomes the Antonyms box or the Related Words box, depending on which one you clicked.

Note: If you chose the last option to experiment and now wish to continue following the practice steps, move to steps 6 and 7 to return to "exciting" as the keyword. Then continue with step 3.

3. Click the Look Up button to have the Thesaurus work with "stimulating." The listing in the Synonyms For box reflects this change.

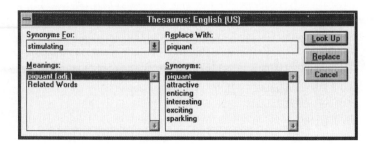

4. Click Related Words in the Meanings box. The word "stimulate" appears in the Related Words box. Click "stimulate," then click Look Up.

5. In the Synonyms box, click "invigorate," then click the Look Up button.

As you can see, you can spend quite a bit of time winding your way down the road of synonyms. If you wish, you can go back to your original word, which was "exciting." Click the down arrow at the right of the Synonyms For box, and a drop-down list box opens.

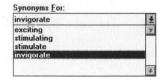

You are looking at a list of all the words you have looked up.

6. Open the Synonyms For drop-down list box and select "exciting."

The dialog box now looks as it did at the beginning of this exercise.

7. Click Replace.

You are returned to the document with the word "stimulating" where "exciting" used to be.

If you wish to look up a word that is not related to anything you're working with, highlight the word that is in the Replace With box, type the word you wish to look up, and click Look Up.

If the word looked up is not a keyword, then a list of words that are alphabetically close to that word appears. For example, if you try to look up the word "diskette," the Thesaurus does not find it.

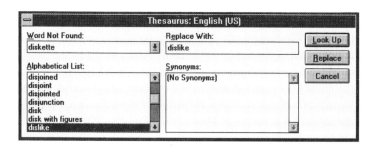

The Synonyms For box is now called Word Not Found, and the Meanings box becomes Alphabetical List.

To practice using the Thesaurus, choose a replacement synonym for "enjoy" at the end of the first sentence in the first paragraph of RAFT-ING2.DOC. Then choose Close from the File menu and do not save the changes.

What Do They Mean By...?

Antonym   A word with an opposite meaning to the keyword.

Keyword   One of the 24,000 words that the Thesaurus recognizes.

Spelling   A Word for Windows feature that checks each word of a document for correct spelling.

Synonym   A word with a similar meaning to the keyword.

Thesaurus   A Word for Windows feature that checks a word for synonyms, antonyms, and any related words.

Four score and seven years

Glossaries—A Great Feature

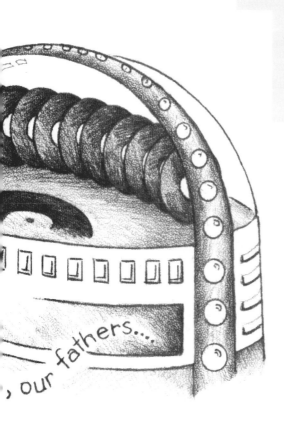

The more you use a word processor, the more you might find yourself using the same words, phrases, sentences, or paragraphs. Typing the identical items over and over can become quite tedious. You could copy the text from one file to another, but that might not actually save you much time.

What Is a Glossary?

Word for Windows does away with this issue by using glossaries. A *glossary* is a place you can store frequently used text and graphics, which you can insert into a document with just a few keystrokes. There is a limit of 16,000 words per glossary entry, with the number of entries limited to available hard-disk space.

Once a glossary entry is created, it is stored in a specific template and is available to any document using the same template. For example, let's say you create a document with the template NORMAL.DOT, and then make a glossary entry while in that document. Any other document with NORMAL.DOT as its template can also use that glossary entry. Documents created with another template cannot use the glossary entries based on NORMAL.DOT. The glossary entry is not tied to a single file, however. Once you create an entry, it is accessible until you delete it.

Note: *For more information on using the other templates included with Word for Windows, take a look at your Word for Windows user's guide.*

A glossary entry can be saved with any formatting available, such as its font, character size, whether the text is centered or bold, and so on.

Why Is a Glossary Used?

Here are some examples of glossary entries:

- Long names that are difficult to spell
- Frequently used mailing addresses
- Standard closings to letters

- Your company name and logo
- Standard contract clauses
- Distribution lists for memos

Think of the time that could be saved by not having to type something like this:

If the standard closing to your letter could be reduced to a glossary entry called Closing, for example, you could already start thinking about your next document.

> If you have any further questions, I can be contacted Monday through Friday between the hours of 8:30 A.M. and 4:30 P.M. My number is 510-555-9876.
>
> Sincerely,

As another example, if you are in the legal profession and need to type standard contracts or copyright notices, each item can be given a glossary name and retrieved at any time.

You can make changes to existing glossary entries and then save the changes.

How to Create a Glossary Entry

For practice, choose New from the File menu. With NORMAL.DOT as the selected template, click on OK.

Type in the name and address from the following illustration, pressing ENTER to separate each line. To create a glossary entry from this text:

1. Highlight all the text you want as the glossary entry, in this case, the entire name and address.

> Mr. Stanley K. Raynell
> Raynell Public Relations
> 55 East 87th Street
> New York, New York 12345

2. Choose Glossary from the Edit menu. The Glossary dialog box appears.

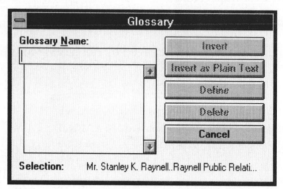

Notice that the first few words of the selected text appear at the bottom of the dialog box, next to Selection. It is a good idea to check this to be sure you are making a glossary entry of the correct text.

The cursor is inside the Glossary Name box. This is where you type the name of the glossary. Until you start typing a glossary name, all command buttons except Cancel are unavailable.

3. Type **skr**.

Note: *Word for Windows is case-insensitive to glossary names.*

4. Click the Define button to go back to the document.

Tip: *A glossary name can be up to 31 characters (including spaces), but you should keep it short so you can retrieve the entry with just a few keystrokes.*

5. To clear the text from the screen, select all the text and press DEL.

How to Insert a Glossary Entry

A glossary entry can be inserted into a document either of two ways: by using the Glossary dialog box or by using keystrokes.

To insert a glossary entry using the Glossary dialog box:

1. Position the cursor on a new line in your document.

2. Choose Glossary from the Edit menu.
   The skr entry appears in the list box below the Glossary Name box. As more entries are created, an alphabetical list of the entries appears in this box.

3. Click skr and click Insert.

The entry is now in the document.

The button called Insert as Plain Text inserts a formatted entry (bold, centered, and so on) without the formatting.

To insert a glossary entry using keyboard equivalents, type the glossary entry name, then press F3.

How to Edit a Glossary Entry

Some glossary entries, such as client mailing addresses, might need to be updated from time to time. You can change a glossary entry without having to type the entire entry again.

For practice changing a glossary entry, follow these steps:

1. Insert the skr glossary entry into a new document.

2. Imagine that the address and company name need to be updated. The name of the company has changed to Smarty Pants Public Relations, and the address is now 60 East 8th Street. Make these changes to the glossary entry you just inserted.

3. Highlight the entire updated glossary entry and choose Glossary from the Edit menu. The text in the Selection area of the dialog box will change to reflect the text change.

4. Click the name skr in the Glossary Name list box, then click Define. A dialog box appears for confirmation of the change in glossary entry text.

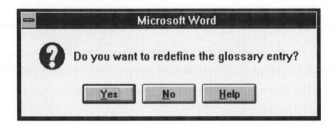

5. Click Yes.

For more practice, modify the text of the Closing glossary entry to make it more suitable to your needs.

How to Delete a Glossary Entry

To delete a glossary entry:

1. Choose Glossary from the Edit menu.

2. Click the entry in the Glossary Entry list box to be deleted.

3. Click the Delete button.

Note: There is no confirming dialog box for the Delete command. If you delete the wrong entry, you must create the entry again.

How to Save a Glossary Entry

When you exit Word for Windows, it asks for confirmation to save any changes you have made to the glossaries.

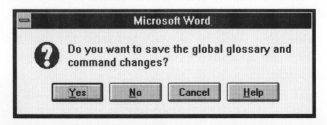

Choosing Yes saves all glossary entries created and modified during that session of Word for Windows, ensuring that the new entries will be available the next time you use the program. Choosing No leaves the glossaries untouched.

Note: Word for Windows can print out on paper the name of each glossary entry along with its text by choosing Print from the File menu and Glossary from the drop-down list box that will appear.

What Do They Mean By...?

Glossary   A Word for Windows feature that allows you to store frequently used words or phrases that can be inserted into a document at any time.

Using Graphics
in Your
Document

Word for Windows has the capability to include graphics within a document. You can either bring in (the Word for Windows term is *import*) graphics created in other programs or create your own graphics using the Microsoft Draw program that comes with Word for Windows. If you wish to learn more about Microsoft Draw (which also edits art imported from other programs), take a look at the Microsoft Draw user's guide included with the Word for Windows documentation.

The term *graphics* in this chapter is used to encompass artwork or pictures created using a drawing program, as well as charts and graphs created using a spreadsheet program.

Importing Word for Windows Graphics

If you opted for a complete installation of Word for Windows, a subdirectory of sample pictures was loaded onto the hard disk at that time. The subdirectory is called CLIPART, and is located within the WINWORD directory. If you did not install the sample graphics and wish to do so for this lesson, refer to the Word for Windows *Getting Started* guide.

How to Insert Graphic Files into Your Document

For practice inserting a graphic, open RAFT-ING2.DOC and place the cursor on the blank line above the third paragraph, which begins: "Unlike most other rivers..."

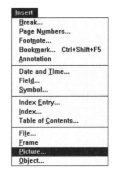

1. Position the cursor at the point you wish to bring in the graphic.

2. Choose Picture from the Insert menu.

3. When the Picture dialog box appears, double-click the CLIPART directory (or single-click, then click OK or press ENTER).

   The files listed under File Name (which displays all the files available to you) change because the active directory is now c:\WINWORD\CLIPART. You can select a graphic from the File Name list, then click the Preview button to see a miniature of the graphic before importing it into your document.

4. Click the graphic named VICHOUSE.WMF, which is a picture of a Victorian-style house.

5. Click the Preview button to see the picture of the house.

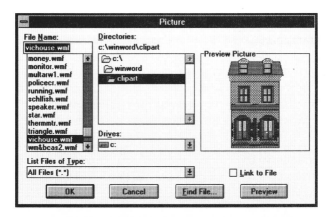

6. Click OK. You are returned to the document.

Note: VICHOUSE.WMF is a color picture. If you do not have a color printer, the graphic will print with shades of grey.

List Files of Type, on the Picture dialog box, is a drop-down list of the different kinds of graphic files that Word for Windows can import. Click the arrow to see this list of file

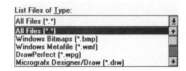

formats. Select All Files (*.*) to view the names of all files regardless of file type.

Here are the types of graphic files that Word for Windows can understand, as well as the file extensions usually associated with them:

Graphic File	Extension	Graphic File	Extension
TIFF (Tagged Image File Format)	TIF	PC Paintbrush	PCX
		Encapsulated Postscript	EPS
Windows Metafile	WMF		
Windows Bitmap	BMP	Computer Graphics Metafile	CGM
HP Graphic Language	HGL		
		Drawperfect	WPG
Lotus 1-2-3 Graphics	PIC	Micrographx Designer 3.0 or Draw Plus	DRW
AutoCAD 2-Dimensional	DXF		
AutoCAD Plotter or Binary ADI	PLT		

Consult the manual for your graphic program to see which file formats it has in common with Word for Windows.

Note: All the sample graphic files supplied by Word for Windows are Windows Metafile (WMF) format.

How to Manipulate Graphic Files

Once the graphic is brought into the document, you can change the size of the graphic, trim (or *crop*) it, add a printable border around it, or change its alignment.

To resize a graphic, the graphic must first be selected by clicking anywhere within the picture. Handles will appear on the picture that (when dragged) will shrink, stretch, or move your graphic.

You may select pieces of your graphic for manipulation by clicking on one of the sizing handles while holding down the SHIFT key.

To place a border around your picture, first select the graphic and then choose Border from the Format menu. A list of design choices (such as shaded background or double-lined box) will be presented for you to choose from.

Note: *Choose Picture from the Format menu to return the graphic to its original proportions.*

What Do They Mean By...?

Sizing handles   Eight small, black squares that appear around a selected graphic.

Crop   Pruning or clipping away the unwanted part of a graphic.

Import   Bringing in or inserting an item into the active document.

Graphics   Artwork created by a drawing program, or charts and graphs created by a spreadsheet program.

Index